54 Years That Changed

1958-2012

By: Pope Michael

"He came unto His own: and His own received Him not. But as many as received Him, He gave them power to be made the sons of God, to them that believe in His name."

- John 1:11-12

Table of Contents

Introduction..5
What Are We Bound To Know?..9
Where Can the Truths of the Divine and Catholic Faith Be Found?..17
    Infallibility of the Councils of the Church............................19
    Extraordinary Magisterium of the Pope...............................20
    Minimizing Infallibility 21
    Professions of Faith..22
    Canon Law..23
    Infallibility of Encyclicals..27
    The Fathers of the Church...28
    Conclusion...29
Sins Against the Faith..30
    Schism..31
    Cum Ex Apostolatus Officio...33
    Apostasy..35
    Heresy..37
    Consequences...40
    A Modern Heresy..42
    Conclusion...44
Passion of the Mystical Body of Christ......................................45
    A Recurring Crisis...46
    Antipopes..50
    The Crisis Begins..51
    Angelo Roncalli...52
Vatican II..56
    The First Heretical Document...58
    What Are the Consequences of This?..................................66
    What of Their Progeny?..68
    Is Allah God?...69
    Are the New Rites of the Sacraments Valid?.......................71
    The Novus Ordo Missae...75
    Surely This Cannot Be True..80
    But My Priest Never Said the Novus Ordo..........................83

- Conclusion 84
- Are Catholics Catholic? 85
  - Is Jesus Really Present? 86
  - The Pedophile Crisis 88
  - Extra Ecclesiam Nulla Salus 91
  - What Does the Catholic Church Teach on Salvation? ... 93
- A Prophetic Overview 97
  - The Worst Time Ever 101
  - Antichrist 102
  - The Holy Sacrifice of the Mass 104
  - Will Cease Entirely For Some Time 104
  - Objections 106
  - Aren't You Speculating? 108
  - Conclusion 109
  - And Another Beast Rose 110
- Reaction to the Changes 113
  - Theories on the Papacy 118
  - Archbishop Peter Martin Ngo-Dihn Thuc 119
  - The Society of Saint Pius X Splits 121
  - The Society Splits Again 122
  - The Indult Mass 123
  - Meanwhile 124
  - Jurisdiction 125
  - Priest Co-Consecrators 127
  - Home Alone 128
  - The Church Comfortable 129
  - Catholic Action 131
- What Is Most Important: 134
- The Mass or the Faith? 134
- The Solution? 138
  - Pope Gregory XVII? 139
  - Papal Claimants 140
- Mission of the Catholic Church 142
  - Habemus Papam 151
- An Urgent Appeal 154
- Professions of Faith 156

    Profession of Faith Prescribed by Pope Michael......................156
    Explanation of the Profession of Faith Prescribed by Pope
    Michael...158
    Profession of Faith of Trent...159
    Oath Against the Errors of Modernism................................162
Appendices...165
    Cum Ex Apostolatus Officio 166
    Insauratio Liturgica..173
    Catechism of the Council of Trent..174
    January 1970 Notice From Rome..175
    May 1970 Notice from Rome..176
    Monseigneur, We Do Not Want This Peace............................180
    Declaration of Archbishop Peter Martin Ngo-Dihn Thuc.....182

Introduction

In the past five decades many things have happened to the Catholic Church from radical changes in doctrine and liturgy to a host of scandals. Surveys show that many who claim to be Catholic do not hold the doctrines taught by the Catholic Church. 88% believe birth control is acceptable and two thirds see nothing wrong with pre-marital sex. And almost half think there is nothing wrong with homosexual practices, while half reject the infallibility of the Pope.

The news regularly echoes scandals among the clergy, especially the ongoing pedophile crisis. Seeing all of this, we cannot do anything, but conclude that there is a crisis in the One, Holy, Catholic, and Apostolic Church. But we know that Jesus promised to be with the Church until the end of time, and that the gates of Hell will not prevail against the Church.[1] We cannot say Jesus failed the Church, but we can say that men have failed Jesus and His Church! This book intends to address these issues.

The first thing Catholics must do is to bring themselves in line with the teachings of Jesus Christ 100%.[2] In fact, if we do not believe everything Jesus teaches through His Church, we are not Catholics, even if we claim to be. We might as well call ourselves wolves in sheep's clothing.[3] It is only in total conformity to the teachings of Jesus that any solution can be found.

To obtain this solution, we must apply the traditions which Christ instituted to the current condition of the Church. In order to properly understand the traditions which Christ

---

1   Matthew 16:18 and 28:19-20
2   "Going therefore, teach ye all nations: baptizing them in the Name of the Father and of the Son and of the Holy Ghost. Teaching them to observe all things whatsoever I have commanded you. And behold I am with you all days, even to the consummation of the world." (Matthew 28:19-20)
3   "Beware of false prophets, who come to you in the clothing of sheep, but inwardly they are ravening wolves." (Matthew 7:15)

instituted, we must seek God with the greatest humility and sincerity. For God resists the proud.[4] And so, we will consider three things.

Firstly we will determine what the teachings of Jesus and His Church are and where they can be found. Secondly, we will analyze the current crisis of the Church. Finally, we will apply the teachings of Jesus and find the solution, a solution that is in total conformity with the doctrines of the Divine and Catholic Faith.

Before proceeding, let us all make a Novena[5] to the Holy Ghost, asking Him to guide us as He has guided Catholics throughout two millennia. Let us apply the talents God has given us to this study of the Faith. Study is what we must do. Jesus foretold that there would be a time when even the elect will be deceived.[6] There will come a time of confusion and ignorance. Fortunately, ignorance is a curable disease. Jesus has established His Church on a firm rock. This will teach us all we need to know to dispel the fog of confusion. In fact, Jesus commanded us to study: "when you see the abomination of desolation in the holy place."[7] The Church has always commanded Catholics to continually study their Faith. It is the virtue of studiousness that cures us of the disease of ignorance and shines the light of faith toward Heaven for us to walk and obtain the precious treasure: eternal salvation. The Church has always encouraged those who are able to read to continually refresh their intellect and mind on the eternal truths and dogmas of the Catholic Faith.

Are we in the times foretold by the Apostle when men

---

4   "God resisteth the proud, and giveth grace to the humble." (James 4:6)

5   "(Latin for ninth, consisting of nine) A prayer for some special object or occasion extended over a period of nine days. It may be carried on in common in Church but is often private. A number of novenas, chiefly in preparation for various feasts, have been approved and indulgenced by the Holy See." (A Catholic Dictionary, Page: 346)

6   Matthew 24:24

7   Matthew 24:15

will not hold to sound doctrine?[8] This book should answer the question in the affirmative. This gives us even more reason to read and understand as Jesus commands.[9] The Blessed Virgin Mary gave us a clue when she commanded the late Lucia dos Santos, one of the Fatima seers, to learn how to read. Whether or not you agree that we are in these times, all Catholics should agree that studying the Faith is not imprudent. What will it profit us if we do not pass our particular judgment of our souls? Studying extra hard for this examination is not careless, but rather sensible and responsible. A look at the last century and a half, also the teachings of the popes should encourage us to study our Faith.[10]

Some may ask: "Why should I believe what you say?" Do not believe what I am saying, but believe what the Church says. If you doubt I have quoted a text properly or out of context, then check it out for yourself. In this presentation, I have tried to use texts that are readily available either in print, on the internet, or at least in good libraries. I am not asking you to take my word for it. Read and understand. Study the question for yourself. It is our responsibility as Catholics to check things out. We must correct each other when we err.

One priest long ago advised to trust only books printed prior to 1958. For the most part I shall refer only to these books. The reason is simple. The confusion appeared to begin in 1958. We can be safer with books printed prior to that time. And a word of caution must be issued about some reprints of older books. Some presses are faithful to the original, while other presses are not. As we continue through, I will point out when I have found people to be unfaithful to the original. In preparing this, I have compiled a sizeable library of original editions of most of the works I refer to. I do have and use reprints, but I have found the publishers I use to be faithful in those works I

---

8   II Timothy 4:3
9   Matthew 24:15
10   Pope Saint Pius X devoted a whole Encyclical to the necessity of studying the Catechism, <u>Acerbo Nimis</u>.

could check out. If you can check a quote I use against an original edition of a work, please do so.

> We would like to thank all of those who helped on this book, who out of the desire of humility, do not wish to be known, but only to God.

> Pope Michael, Servant of the Servants of God.

Chapter 1
What Are We Bound To Know?

"Going therefore, teach ye all nations: baptizing them in the name of the Father and of the Son and of the Holy Ghost. Teaching them to observe all things whatsoever I have commanded you. And behold I am with you all days, even to the consummation of the world."[11]

Jesus gave these commands to the Apostles before ascending into Heaven. If the Apostles and their successors are bound to teach us all the things that Jesus taught them, then we are bound to learn these things in order to obtain salvation.

"When therefore you shall see the abomination of desolation, which was spoken of by Daniel the prophet, standing in the holy place: he that readeth let him understand."[12] Jesus foretold in the Gospels certain events that would one day befall the Church and the world.[13] For there shall arise false Christs and false prophets and shall shew great signs and wonders, insomuch as to deceive (if possible) even the elect.[14]

"For there will rise up false Christs and false prophets: and they shall shew signs and wonders, to seduce (if it were possible) even the elect."[15] This is quoted from three different Gospels. This is to show the extent of the deception that will come at some time in history. "And when you shall see the abomination of desolation, standing where it ought not (he that readeth let him understand): then let them that are in Judea flee unto the mountains."[16] Jesus gives us a remedy for deception. Study the truths of the Faith from sources we can be certain are

---

11 Mathew 28:19-20
12 Matthew 24:15
13 Matthew 24: Mark 13; Luke 21
14 Matthew 24:24
15 Mark 13:22
16 Mark 13:14

accurate. These false prophets will be so crafty as to deceive even the elect! Subsequently, we are morally obliged to flee from places that are preaching dangerous doctrines such as heresy.

We have a choice among various resources for information. It is reasonable to use those sources we are sure are correct. It is also reasonable to be opposed to those we are not sure of. If a book is published by a younger or modern person, its opinion should be considered as probable, since it is not established that it has been rejected by the Holy See as improbable.[17] Pope Alexander VII condemned this proposition on September 24, 1665. So let us rephrase this proposition to be a true one. We should not consider an opinion valuable, merely because the Church has not yet condemned it.[18]

These questions arise: "Are we in these times when we must read and study?" Has the abomination of desolation been placed in the Holy Place? These are both complicated questions. Let us look at a few small things, leaving the larger questions for later. The Blessed Virgin Mary at Fatima (1917) commanded Lucia dos Santos to learn how to read. Pope Saint Pius X feared in 1903 that Antichrist had already been born.[19] These two things should at least be warnings that we may be in these times. Therefore, we must devote ourselves to study.

Saint John Vianney, the holy Cure of Ars told his people:

> "A good Christian is not satisfied to simply believe
> in the truths of our holy religion. He loves them,
> he ponders over them, he tries in every possible

---

17   The Sources Of Catholic Dogma, # 1127, Page: 321
18   Now the question arises, what of this work here, which is obviously new. We ask the reader to check out and verify the accuracy of every source for themselves. Follow the reasoning. Only accept it if it is obviously true, and in accord with Catholic doctrine. We also ask the reader to apply the exact same level of work to anything written in the past half a century.
19   E Supremi, his first Encyclical. There is an intimate connection between Antichrist and the Abomination of Desolation. This is because Antichrist sets up the Abomination of Desolation.

way to acquire a knowledge of them; he loves to hear the word of God, and the more he hears it, the more he longs for it."[20]

Pope Saint Pius X gave pastors strict instructions:

"Since it is a fact that in these days adults need instruction no less than the young, all pastors and those having the care of souls shall explain the Catechism to the people in a plain and simple style adapted to the intelligence of their hearers. This shall be carried out on all holy days of obligation, at such time as is most convenient for the people, but not during the same hour when the children are instructed, and this instruction must be in addition to the usual homily on the Gospel which is delivered at the parochial Mass on Sundays and holy days. The catechetical instruction shall be based on the Catechism of the Council of Trent; and the matter is to be divided in such a way that in the space of four or five years, treatment will be given to the Apostles' Creed, the Sacraments, the Ten Commandments, the Lord's Prayer and the Precepts of the Church."[21]

Looking back at the last century, it should be obvious that this command of Pope Saint Pius X has been almost totally ignored. Although our pastors sinned seriously in neglecting this responsibility, it does not absolve us from our responsibility to learn the truths of the Faith. This responsibility comes from the Divine law!

Pope Clement XIII[22] wrote almost 250 years ago:

---

20 Sermons of the Cure of Ars, Page: 269
21 Acerbo nimis, Paragraph 24, 15 April 1905
22 In Dominico agro, 14 June 1761

"As our predecessors understood that that holy meeting of the universal Church[23] was so prudent in judgment and so moderate that it abstained from condemning ideas which authorities among Church scholars supported, they wanted another work prepared with the agreement of that holy council which would cover the entire teaching which the faithful should know and which would be far removed from any error. They printed and distributed this book under the title of the Roman Catechism."[24]

He began this particular encyclical with the following paragraph:

"In the Lord's field, for the tending of which Divine Providence placed Us as overseer, there is nothing which demands as much vigilant care and unremitting labor in its cultivation than guarding the good seed of Catholic teaching which the Apostles received from Jesus Christ and handed on to Us. If in laziness this is neglected, the enemy of the human race will sow weeds while the workers sleep. Then weeds will be found which should be committed to the flames rather than good grain to store in the barns."[25]

Pope Pius IX addressed the bishops in the papal states and asked them to deal with teachers as follows:

"Advise these men that when they are instructing, to keep in view the Roman Catechism, which was published by a decree of the Council of Trent and

---

23   The Council of Trent
24   Catechism of the Council of Trent
25   In Dominico Agro, Pope Clement XIII, Paragraph 1

the order of Saint Pius V Our Predecessor of immortal memory."

Other supreme pontiffs, to name one, Clement XIII of happy memory, recommended this book as, "a most suitable aid for removing the deceits of bad opinions and for spreading and establishing true and sound doctrine."[26]

The <u>Roman Catechism</u>, also known as the <u>Catechism of the Council of Trent</u>, was written by order of the Council of Trent for pastors to use in their teaching. In various countries, the bishops have commissioned simpler catechisms for use by children and young adults. In the United States, the Councils of Baltimore ordered catechisms prepared.[27] All of these catechisms should be in our libraries. These catechisms should also be regularly in our hands and studied. They form a basis of the Faith from which to build on.

We must remember that the catechism is a summary of what we must know and do to be Catholics. The catechism should be our constant companion. We recommend that all know the <u>Roman Catechism</u> because pastors are supposed to bring us up to this level of knowledge. This recommendation is made to all adult Catholics. In this presentation we will rely not only on the <u>Roman Catechism</u>, but other catechisms to lay the foundation on which to build. As Deharbe's Catechism observes in the introduction:

> "Catechetical instruction, Pius X observes, is the basis of all other kinds of religious instruction. Catechism is merely the beginning. When doctrine is questioned, all are called on to learn more about the doctrine. We are to accept the teachings of the Divine and Catholic Faith without

---

26   <u>Notis et Nobiscum</u>, Paragraph 30, 8 December 1849. Quotes are from <u>In Dominico agro</u>.
27   The first edition is in reprint. I do not recommend the newer editions. They have been simplified.

question! When we follow the basic principle of scholastic theology,[28] we shall move from what we all should know well (i.e. the Catechism), to what we do not know yet."[29]

Saint John Vianney reminds us in his catechism to his people:

"Saint Charles Borromeo tells us explicitly that absolution cannot be given to persons who do not know the principle facts of the Christian Religion, and the responsibilities of their state of life; particularly when their ignorance arises from their indifference concerning their salvation. The laws of the Church in this connection also forbid absolution to be given to fathers or mothers who do not teach children, or have them taught, in everything that is necessary for their salvation."[30]

Catholics are bound to know the truths of the Faith and to teach these truths to their children. Then Saint John Vianney warns us: "We shall find out at the day of judgment that the greater number of Christians who are lost were damned because

---

28   Scholasticism is "The philosophy that flourished during the middle ages and which is personified in the Dominican Saint Thomas Aquinas. It is the philosophy of the Fathers reduced to a grand synthesis and presented in a didactic form. To give a precise definition of Scholasticism is difficult, but it would seem to be a spirit whereby an endeavor is made (by the Fathers of the Church and their successors) to bring into harmony faith and reason. A didactic method, derived especially from Aristotle's philosophy, such as is a necessary to establish the aforesaid harmony. A system, always susceptible of further development, the foundations of which are to be discovered in the works of Saint Thomas Aquinas. The name is derived from Latin, scholasticus, the title given to the masters of the Christian schools of the early middle ages." (A Catholic Dictionary, Page: 452)
29   Scholasticism is the method of study approved by the Catholic Church, and praised by many Popes.
30   Sermons of the Cure of Ars, Page: 240

they did not know their own religion."[31]

And a word must be said of the responsibilities of the clergy. The laity are bound to know the catechism and more. How much more should the clergy know? Pastors are commanded to teach their flocks from the <u>Roman Catechism</u>. Therefore, it is reasonable to conclude that every priest should read the <u>Roman Catechism</u> cover to cover. At the ordination of lectors, the bishop admonishes them:

> "Study, therefore, to announce distinctly and clearly the words of God, that is, the holy Lessons, for the understanding and edification of the faithful. Do not falsify the text lest the truth of the Divine Lessons intended for the instruction of your hearers, should through your carelessness be corrupted. And what you read with your lips, believe in your hearts and practice by your works, so that you may be able to teach your hearers equally by word and example."[32]

Lectors read the lessons from the Breviary and some from the Missal in Church. They also should be ready to teach the Catechism to the faithful as assistants to the priests. The Fourth Lateran Council tells us: "Ignorance is the mother of all errors."[33]

And a catechism prepared to help parish priests tells us:

> "Ignorance of Catholic doctrine is the cause of most of the bigotry and misunderstanding found among non-Catholics. Ignorance of their own religion among Catholics themselves is largely responsible for the unworthy Catholics whom worldliness estranges from God and the practice of

---

31 <u>Sermons of the Cure of Ars</u>, Page: 99
32 <u>Pontificale Romanum</u>, translation from <u>The Rite of Ordination</u>
33 <u>Humani Generis Redemptionem</u>, Pope Benedict XV, Paragraph 14

religions responsibilities. Even practical and devout Catholics need constant instruction lest they should stumble into serious doctrinal error."[34]

Fortunately, ignorance is a curable disease.

---

[34] <u>A Parochial Course in Doctrinal Instruction</u>, Page: 4

Chapter 2
Where Can the Truths of the Divine and Catholic Faith Be Found?

"124. Q. What do you mean by the infallibility of the Church? A. By the infallibility of the Church, I mean that the Church cannot err when it teaches a doctrine of faith or morals. **Infallibility.** When we say the Church is infallible, we mean that it cannot make a mistake or err in what it teaches; that the Pope, the head of the Church, is infallible when he teaches Ex cathedra -- that is, as the successor of Saint Peter, the vicar of Christ. Cathedra signifies a seat, Ex stands for **out of**; therefore, Ex cathedra means out of the chair or office of Saint Peter. Chair is sometimes used for office. Thus, we say the presidential chair is opposed to this or that. We intend to say the president, or the one in that office is opposed to it. The cathedral is the church in which the bishop usually officiates. The cathedral is called this because of the bishop's cathedra, or throne, being in it." [35]

"125. Q. When does the Church teach infallibly? A. The Church teaches infallibly when it speaks through the Pope and bishops united in general council, or through the Pope alone when he proclaims to all the faithful a doctrine of faith or morals. How will we know when the Pope speaks Ex cathedra, when he is speaking daily to people from all parts of the world? To speak Ex cathedra or infallibly, three things are required: "He must speak as the head of the whole Church, not as a private person; and in certain forms of words by

---

[35] The Baltimore Catechism, Page: 118

which we know he is speaking Ex cathedra. What he says must hold good for the whole Church. That is for all the faithful, and not merely for this or that particular person or country. He must speak on matters of faith or morals. That is: when the Holy Father tells all the faithful that they are to believe a certain thing as a part of their faith, or when he tells them that certain things are sins. They must believe him and avoid what he declares to be sin. He could not make a mistake in such things. He could not say that Our Lord taught us to believe and do such and such if Our Lord did not so teach. Our Lord promised to be with His Church for all time. Our Lord also promised to send the Holy Ghost, who would teach all truth and abide with it forever. If the Church could make mistakes in teaching faith and morals, the Holy Ghost could not dwell within Her. This is equivalent to saying Our Lord did not tell us the truth, and to say this would be blasphemy."[36]

---

36   The Baltimore Catechism, Page: 119

Infallibility of the Councils of the Church

The Church has had 20 General or Ecumenical[37] Councils. The first Council was held at Nicea.[38] The last Council was at the Vatican.[39] These decrees become infallible the moment they are approved by the Pope. The Council deliberates on the questions submitted for consideration when the Pope calls it. The Council then issues decrees and submits them to the Pope for approval. Many Councils were not presided over by the Pope, but by his legates. The last Council was presided over personally by Pope Pius IX. We can be certain that everything from these Councils are true and in full accord with the Divine and Catholic Faith.

---

37 "Ecumenical Councils are those to which the bishops, and others entitled to vote, are convoked from the whole world (oikoumene) under the presidency of the pope or his legates, and the decrees of which, having received papal confirmation, bind all Christians. A council, Ecumenical in its convocation, may fail to secure the approbation of the whole Church or of the pope, and thus not rank in authority with Ecumenical councils. Such was the case with the Robber Synod of 449 (Latrocinium Ephesinum), the Synod of Pisa in 1409, and in part with the Councils of Constance and Basle." (Catholic Encyclopedia, Volume 4, Page: 424)
38 325 A.D.
39 1870 A.D.

Extraordinary Magisterium of the Pope

Many think the Pope is only infallible when solemnly surrounded by Cardinals and Bishops and sufficient incense wafts our prayers to Heaven. Then, the Pope pronounces on a doctrine of Faith or Morals in an extraordinary manner. This of course has happened throughout history, when the doctrines of the Assumption in 1950 and the Immaculate Conception in 1846 were defined. These are certainly doctrines of faith which the Pope has solemnly and infallibly defined.

Prior to 1958, a book was published listing documents the author considered infallible. In the past century and a half, in addition to the two definitions above, the Syllabus of Errors issued by Pope Pius IX[40] and the Syllabus of Modernist Errors condemned by Pope Saint Pius X were included.[41] Casti Conubii of Pope Pius XI on Christian Marriage was also included as was Quadragesimo Anno, commemorating the 40th anniversary of Rerum Novarum, (which for some reason was omitted from this list).

Some would have us stop here and consider everything else emanating from the Pope as not being preserved in any way by infallibility.

---

40 The Sources Of Catholic Dogma, # 1688-1699, Pages: 429-433
41 The Sources Of Catholic Dogma, # 2239-2250, Pages: 590-597
  The Sources Of Catholic Dogma, # 2253-2333, Pages: 598-648

Minimizing Infallibility

Fr. Le Floch, head of the French seminary in Rome in 1926 taught: "The heresy which is now being born will become the most dangerous of all; the exaggeration of the respect due to the Pope and the illegitimate extension of his infallibility." Fr. Le Floch was trying to minimize the doctrine of infallibility, by stating that the next heresy will try to expand infallibility. This is a typical Gallican idea. Before the ink was even dry on the decrees of the Vatican Council in 1870, many were trying to limit Papal infallibility to such rare occurrence as to be almost non-existent. Some reduced it to three times in the last two centuries. Namely: The Immaculate Conception, Infallibility, and The Assumption. Others expanded infallibility more by representing the list referred to above. Does Papal Infallibility go any further? We have not exhausted the list of those things emanating from the extraordinary magisterium[42] of the Church. However, the Church is also infallible in its ordinary magisterium,[43] which we shall consider in a moment.

---

42 "The solemn magisterium is that which is exercised only rarely by formal and authentic definitions of councils or popes. Its matter comprises dogmatic definitions of ecumenical councils or of the popes teaching **ex cathedra**, or of particular councils, if their decrees are universally accepted or approved in solemn form by the pope. Also creeds and professions of faith put forward or solemnly approved by pope or ecumenical council." (A Catholic Dictionary, Page: 301)

43 "The ordinary magisterium is continually exercised by the Church especially her universal practices connected with faith and morals, in the unanimous consent of the Fathers and theologians, in the decisions of Roman Congregations concerning faith and morals, in the common sense of the faithful, and various historical documents in which the faith is declared. All these are founts of a teaching which as a whole is infallible. They have to be studied separately to determine how far and in what conditions each of them is an infallible source of truth." (A Catholic Dictionary, Page: 301)

Professions of Faith

All should be familiar with the Profession of Faith issued by the Council of Trent in 1565, and modified by the Vatican Council in 1870. This Profession of Faith is ordered for bishops before their consecration. This Profession of Faith is also ordered for baptized people when they convert to the Catholic Faith, and are absolved from any excommunication they may have incurred for heresy.[44]

We can consider the Apostles' Creed upon which part of the Catechism is patterned as the first Profession of Faith. In fact, a child was asked what he believed and he simply recited the Apostles' Creed. Indeed, this child was correct. The next time we recite the Rosary, we should stop and think that we are professing our Catholic Faith as we begin.

However, the Apostles' Creed is by no means the only Profession of Faith. The Pope has prescribed Professions of Faith for various heretics, which are aimed against their heresies. These very words: **profession of faith**, should be sufficient to tell us that these Professions are infallible.

Let us look at the Profession written by Pope Benedict XIV and prescribed for the Orientals:

> "Likewise, all other things I accept and profess, which the Holy Roman Church accepts and professes, and I likewise condemn, reject, and anathematize, at the same time all contrary things, both schisms and heresies, which have been condemned by the same Church."[45]

And these words echo the simple Act of Faith we should recite daily as found in our basic catechisms.[46]

---

44   The Sources Of Catholic Dogma, # 994-1000, Page: 302-304
45   The Sources Of Catholic Dogma, # 1473, Page: 360
46   Since many have memorized these and they vary slightly, no form will be given here.

Canon Law

We now leave the extraordinary magisterium and go to the ordinary magisterium. The teaching authority of the Church.

> "And I say to thee: That thou art Peter; and upon this rock I will build My church, and the gates of Hell shall not prevail against it. And I will give to thee the keys of the kingdom of Heaven. And whatsoever thou shalt bind upon Earth, it shall be bound also in Heaven: and whatsoever thou shalt loose on Earth, it shall be loosed also in Heaven."[47]

It should be noted that Sacred Scripture is infallibly true, which shall be considered in more detail in a moment.

Jesus told Saint Peter, though him and his successors to the papacy: "whatsoever thou shalt bind upon Earth, it shall be bound also in Heaven." How does the Pope bind? The Pope is the lawgiver of ecclesiastical law (ie canon law) signifying the power to loosen and binding Heaven and Earth to His divine laws (ie dogmas). These are the laws that are made for the Church as a whole, or for each particular Rite.[48]

Let us read from Charles Augustine's <u>A Commentary on Canon Law</u>:[49]

> "Now, the Church Catholic being founded by our Lord and perpetuated by the Apostles and their

---

47   Matthew 16:18-19
48   "A whole and complete system of forms ceremonies and prayers to be used in the worship of God, the administration of the Sacraments, and minor ecclesiastical occasions. The Catholic Church recognizes nine rites, each one of which has its ow right and proper way of doing things, from celebrating the Holy Eucharist downwards. They are: the Latin (including variants), Byzantine, Armenian, Chaldean, Coptic, Ethiopic, Malabar, Maronite, and Syrian rites." (<u>A Catholic Dictionary</u>, Page: 434)
49   <u>A Commentary on Canon Law</u>, Volume 1, Page: 10

lawful successors, among whom the Roman Pontiff holds not only an honorary but also a jurisdictional supremacy, the following must be acknowledged as ecclesiastical lawgivers: "Christ our Lord, the original source of divine laws laid down chiefly in the Constitution of the Church, and next to Him the Apostles as lawgivers either of divine or human laws, viz.: as inspired or merely human instruments. The Roman Pontiff, either alone or in unison with a general council, as endowed with the supreme and ordinary power of enacting laws for the universal church. The Bishops for their respective districts, inasmuch as they are empowered to enact laws subordinate to common law. Customs, too, must be considered as a source of law, universal as well as particular."

Fr. Augustine continues in subsequent pages to list the fontes or sources of Canon Law:[50]

- Sacred Scripture
- Decrees of the Roman Pontiffs
- Canons of Councils
- Unwritten law

Pope Benedict XV issued a decree when promulgating what is now known as the 1917 Code of Canon Law.[51] He calls Canon Law written reason. He concludes:

> "Therefore, having invoked the aid of Divine grace, and relying upon the authority of the Blessed Apostles Peter and Paul, of Our own accord and with certain knowledge, and in the fullness of the

---

50 A Commentary On Canon Law, Volume 1, Page: 10
51 Providentissimus, Pentecost, 1917

Apostolic power with which we are invested, by this Our Constitution, which we wish to be valid for all time, We promulgate, decree, and order that the present Code, just as it is compiled, shall have from this time forth the power of law for the Universal Church..."[52]

Thus, Pope Benedict XV is invoking the fullness of his Apostolic Authority. Therefore, the 1917 Code of Canon Law is binding on the Universal Church. Another conclusion immediately arises. If the Code of Canon Law decrees something that is a matter of Faith or Morals, it is infallible and further the other provisions cannot contradict doctrine. Therefore, Canon Law enjoys at least a negative infallibility.[53]

A doctrine restated in the Code of Canon Law is contained in Canon 815: "The bread must be made of pure wheaten flour, and it must be recently baked so that there is no danger of corruption. The wine must be the natural juice of the grape vine and uncorrupted."[54]

To enable us to learn the authority of various Canons, the Code of Canon Law in the Latin is provided with Fontes. The Code of Canon Law is to be interpreted in the context of Canon Law as it has existed for centuries and even millennia. The Fontes are the sources of Canon Law, the previous laws on which the current canon law is based. These Fontes are taken from the Bulls and Encyclicals of previous Popes, and the decrees of

---

[52] This wording is similar to that found in the Bull of Pope Saint Pius V, Quo primum promulgating the Missale Romanum for use by the Church until the end of time.

[53] Negative Infallibility: "Negative infallibility is the proposition that the Pope cannot commit public formal heresy. Therefore his official statements in Encyclicals and other public documents although not necessarily a definition of the Divine and Catholic Faith (de fide), they are free from error in regards to the Faith and therefore may be safely believed by Catholics as true."

[54] A Practical Commentary On The Code Of Canon Law, Volume 1, Canon 815, Page: 437

General Councils of the Church, etc.

Many of the Canons are merely restatements of previously defined doctrines. This example is taken from the Vatican Council:

> "But, since, it is not sufficient to shun heretical iniquity unless these errors are also shunned which come more or less close to it, we remind all of the responsibility of observing also the constitutions and decrees by which base opinions of this sort, which are not enumerated explicitly here, have been proscribed and prohibited by this Holy See."[55]

Amleto Cicognani in Canon Law teaches:

> "However, on account of the divine assistance which Christ promised His Church, no disciplinary law at variance with orthodox faith[56] or good morals has ever been or ever will be issued by the Roman Pontiff for the universal Church."

From this we can see that God will protect the Church from issuing a general law that will contradict the Catholic Faith. This is only reasonable, since the Church is a divine institution founded to lead all souls to Heaven.

---

55   The Sources Of Catholic Dogma, # 1820, Page: 451
56   "(From the Greek meaning right believer). In common speech, orthodox as an adjective is used of those who profess true doctrine in all its integrity in reference to some standard, named or implied. In this sense the word is used by the Catholic Church in official pronouncements (ie. In the oath against Modernism) and the liturgy (ie. In the prayer Te igitur of the Mass) in reference to the true faith of the Church." (A Catholic Dictionary, Page: 360)

Infallibility of Encyclicals

"Nor must it be thought that what is contained in encyclical letters does not of itself demand assent, on the pretext that the popes do not exercise in them the supreme power of their teaching authority. Rather, such teachings belong to the ordinary magisterium, of which it is true to say: 'He who hears you hears Me.' (Luke 10:16); for the most part, too, what is expounded and inculcated in encyclical letters already appertains to Catholic doctrine for other reasons. But if the supreme pontiffs in their official documents purposely pass judgment on a matter debated until then, it is obvious to all that the matter according to the mind and the will of the same pontiffs, cannot be considered any longer a question open for discussion among theologians."[57]

According to one list, there are 262 encyclicals from the time Popes began writing Encyclicals until the death of Pope Pius XII. Much of what is said in Encyclicals, therefore, is infallible. In any case, it is rash to contradict any of these things. Encyclicals cannot contradict the Catholic Faith.

---

57   Humani Generis, Pope Pius XII, Paragraph 20

The Fathers of the Church

In the Profession of Faith of the Council of Trent, we vow: "I shall never accept or interpret it (Sacred Scripture) otherwise than in accordance with the unanimous consent of the Fathers."[58] The Council of Trent[59] and the Lateran Council[60] confirm that when the Fathers of the Church are unanimous in their teaching of the meaning of a text of Sacred Scripture, they are infallible. It is not necessary that each Father has addressed a particular text, but that the majority have addressed it, and are in unanimous agreement in the proper interpretation. An example of this can be found in the Roman Catechism: "That this visible head" (i.e. Pope) "is necessary to establish and preserve unity in the Church is the unanimous accord of the Fathers."[61]

---

58   The Sources Of Catholic Dogma, # 995, Page: 303
59   The Sources Of Catholic Dogma, # 786, Page: 245
60   The Sources Of Catholic Dogma, # 270, Page: 104
61   Catechism of the Council of Trent, Page: 74

Conclusion

We have determined where we can find the truth, the whole truth, and nothing but the truth. This was infallibly guaranteed by our Lord Jesus Christ when he founded His Church upon the firm rock of the Papacy. Not only that, we have also found out what Jesus is commanding through His representative on Earth, the Vicar of Christ. These decrees of the Church are not mere opinions. These decrees are reserved to theologians and canonists when they discuss the finer points of law and doctrine upon which the Church has not yet pronounced a final decision, namely from the Roman Pontiff.

Chapter 3
Sins Against the Faith

"Finally, the Holy Fathers teach unanimously not only that heretics are outside of the Church, but also that they are **ipso facto**[62] deprived of all ecclesiastical jurisdiction and dignity."[63] Pope Pius XII also infallibly declared: "For not every sin, however great it may be, is such as of its own nature to sever a man from the Body of the Church, as does schism or heresy or apostasy."[64] There are three distinct sins to consider: Schism, apostasy, and heresy.

---

62   Ipso facto: (Latin by that very fact). "A phrase used when expressing that a certain consequence automatically follows a certain action or set of circumstances; e.g., a priest who with full knowledge of the crime and its penalty directly violates the seal of confession incurs excommunication **ipso facto**, by that very fact, automatically, without sentence of law." (A Catholic Dictionary, Page: 261)
63   De Romano Pontifice, Book II, Chapter 30
64   Mystici Corporis Christi, Pope Pius XII, Paragraph 23

Schism

The Code of Canon Law declares: "if, finally, he refuses to be subject to the Supreme Pontiff, or to have communication with the members of the church subject to the Pope, he is a schismatic."[65] Some might object that schism as defined here is not a sin against the Faith. The same Canon defines what an apostate and a heretic is because schism usually leads to heresy. Let us read what the Baltimore Catechism says:

> "A schismatic is one who believes everything the Church teaches, but will not submit to the authority of its head - the Holy Father...Such persons do not long remain only schismatics; for once they rise up against the authority of the Church, they soon reject some of its doctrines and thus become heretics; and indeed, since the Vatican Council, all schismatics are heretics."[66]

Saint John Chrysostom says: "Therefore I assert and protest, that to make a schism in the Church is no less an evil than to fall into heresy."[67] And Saint Jerome says: "Every schism fabricates a heresy for itself to justify its withdrawal from the Church."[68]

"There is nothing more grievous than the sacrilege of schism...there can be no just necessity for destroying the unity of the Church."[69] Saint Cyprian says: "Heresies and schisms have no other origin than that obedience is refused to the priest of God, and that men lose sight of the fact that there is one judge in

---

65   A Practical Commentary On The Code Of Canon Law, Volume 2, Canon 1325, Page: 109
66   Baltimore Catechism Number 4, Q. 323, Page: 267
67   Nicene And Post-Nicene Fathers, Volume 13, Page: 107
68   Quartus Supra, Pope Pius IX, Paragraph 13
69   Contra Epistolam Parmeniani, Saint Augustine, Lib. 2, Cap. 2, N. 25

the place of Christ in this world"[70] Saint Thomas Aquinas says: "The unity of the Church is manifested in the mutual connection or communication of its members, and likewise in the relation of all the members of the Church to one head."[71]

Finally, Saint Cyprian says: "He who deserts the Church will vainly believe that he is in the Church."[72] Schismatics are outside of the Church as infallibly defined by Pope Pius XII.

70	Satis Cognitum, Pope Leo XIII, Paragraph 15
71	Summa Theologica, Saint Thomas Aquinas, II-II, Q. 39, A. 9, Ad. 1
72	Amantissimus, Pope Pius IX, Paragraph 3

Cum Ex Apostolatus Officio

This Bull of Pope Paul IV deserves special consideration, especially in light of the fact that it has been ignored by many. In fact, even Henry Denzinger, in compiling the collection of things pertaining to the Faith omitted this document. He may have omitted it because when a Council was sitting, as Trent was at this time, he omits decrees issuing from the Pope at that time. However, this Bull appears in the Fontes of the Code of Canon Law in several places. It is considered infallible because it teaches on a matter of Faith; that is the consequences of heresy. Let us quote from the most important paragraph, number 6:

> "Adding that if at any time it shall appear that some bishop, even conducting himself as an archbishop or patriarch or already mentioned cardinal of the Roman Church, even, as shown, a legate, or even a Roman Pontiff, before his promotion or assumption as cardinal or as Roman Pontiff had deviated from the Catholic Faith or fallen into some heresy **or incurred, encouraged or incited schism**, before his promotion or assumption as Cardinal or as Roman Pontiff, that promotion or assumption concerning him, even if made in concord and from the unanimous assent of all the cardinals, is null, void and worthless; not by the reception of consecration, not by the ensuing possession of the office and administration, or as if, either the enthronement or homage of the Roman Pontiff, or the obedience given to him by all, and the length of whatever time in the future, can be said to have recovered power or to be able to recover power, nor can (the assumption or promotion) be considered as legitimate in any way, and for those who are promoted as bishops or archbishops or patriarchs

or assumed as primates, or as cardinals or even as Roman Pontiff, no faculty of administration in spiritual or temporal matters may be thought to have been attributed or to attribute, but may all things and each thing in any way said, done, effected and administered and then followed up in any way through them lack power and they are not able to attribute any further power nor right to anyone; and they themselves who are thus promoted and assumed by that very fact, without any further declaration to be made, are deprived of every dignity, place, honor, title, authority, function and power; and yet it is permitted to all and each so promoted and assumed, if they have not deviated from the Faith before nor have been heretics, **nor have incurred or excited or committed schism.**"

Notice that I have put some words in bold letters. To date, I have found five English translations of this Bull. Each translation omits these words! So, when we take the Latin original and prepare a translation based on that, we reinsert these words in their proper place. Not only does <u>Cum Ex Apostolatus Officio</u> define the consequences of heresy, but also of schism. These consequences flow naturally into Canon Law.

Apostasy

The Code of Canon Law says: "Any baptized person who...if he abandons the Christian faith entirely, he is called an apostate."[73] It should be obvious to see that if someone abandons the Faith entirely, he is no longer a member of the Church. Let us say that I am a member of a club and I stop paying dues, and I completely sever all association with the club. They are right to presume I no longer wish to be a member. Simply put, apostates completely depart from the Church.

The Holy Office on the 28th of June, 1949 answered the following question:

> "Whether the faithful who profess the materialistic and anti-Christian doctrine of Communists, and especially those who defend or propagate it, incur **ipso facto** as apostates from the Catholic faith the excommunication specially reserved to the Holy See. In the affirmative. On the following Thursday, the 30th of the same month and year, His Holiness by divine Providence Pope Pius XII, in the customary audience granted to the Most Excellent and Most Reverend Assessor of the Holy Office, approved and ordered that it be promulgated in the official Commentary, Acta Apostolicae Sedis."[74]

Therefore, to be a Communist is to be considered an apostate. What if a Communist infiltrated the Church in order to become a priest?[75] Wouldn't he still be an apostate?

---

73 A Practical Commentary On The Code Of Canon Law, Volume 2, Canon 1325, Page: 109
74 Canon Law Digest, Volume 3, Page: 658
75 A book AA-1025 was published which claims to recount such an infiltration, although newer repents indicate this is a mere work of fiction. We recommend reading The True Story of AA-1025 from Saint Pius X Press

Certainly. His first loyalty is to Communism. He is only pretending to be a Catholic in order to infiltrate the Church. His most probable intention is to destroy the Church. Of the Modernists, Pope Saint Pius X warned:

> "For, as We have said, they put their designs for her (the Church's) ruin into operation not from without but from within; hence, the danger is present almost in the very veins and heart of the Church, whose injury is the more certain, the more intimate is their knowledge of her. Moreover they lay their axes not at the branches and shoots, but to the very root, that is, to the faith and its deepest fibers..."[76]

Apostasy is a total abandonment of the Divine and Catholic Faith. In ages past apostates were presumed also to abandon all appearance of Catholicity, departing entirely from the Catholic Church. What if apostates abandoned the Faith in their hearts while retaining the appearance of Catholicity with the perfidious intention of destroying the Church? "Having an appearance indeed of godliness but denying the power thereof. Now these avoid."[77] What are we to think of these wolves in sheep's clothing?[78] If one reads The True Story of AA-1025, Pascendi or The Permanent Instruction of the Alta Vendita, one finds that men have entered the Church with the sole intention of becoming priests and bishops in order to destroy the Church. These men are indeed wolves in sheep's clothing!

---

76 Pascendi, Pope Saint Pius X, Paragraph 3
77 II Timothy 3:5
78 Matthew 7:15

Heresy

The Vatican Council infallibly teaches:

"Further, by divine and Catholic faith, all those things must be believed which are contained in the written word of God and in tradition, and those which are proposed by the Church, either by solemn pronouncement or in her ordinary and universal teaching power, are to be believed as divinely revealed."[79]

The Code of Canon Law states:

"The faithful are bound to profess their faith publicly, whenever silence, subterfuge, or their manner of acting would otherwise entail an implicit denial of their faith, a contempt of religion, an insult to God, or scandal to their neighbor. Any baptized person who, while retaining the name of Christian, obstinately denies or doubts any of the truths proposed for belief by the divine and Catholic faith, is a heretic; if he abandons the Christian faith entirely, he is called an apostate; if, finally, he refuses to be subject to the Supreme Pontiff, or to have communication with the members of the church subject to the Pope, he is a schismatic."[80]

Let us consider the definition of a heretic: "Any baptized person who, while retaining the name of Christian, **obstinately** denies or doubts any of the truths proposed for belief by the divine and Catholic faith, is a heretic..." I have highlighted the

---

[79] The Sources Of Catholic Dogma, # 1792, Page: 445
[80] A Practical Commentary On The Code Of Canon Law, Volume 2, Canon 1325, Page: 109

word obstinately because many have stressed this word. The Code of Canon Law must judge matters based upon what is seen. It cannot judge the soul. The judgment of the soul is left to God, and to the Confessional when a person voluntarily confesses his sins in order to obtain absolution. We must return to the Bull <u>Cum Ex Apostolatus Officio</u>, which is a Fontes for this Canon: "Adding that if at any time it shall appear that some bishop, ... had deviated from the Catholic Faith or fallen into some heresy or incurred, encouraged or incited schism..." The mere appearance of heresy is sufficient to be considered a heretic in the eyes of the Church. This principle is also enunciated in the Code of Canon Law itself:

> "The evil will, spoken of in Canon 2199, means a deliberate will to violate a law, and presupposes on the part of the mind a knowledge of the law and on the part of the will freedom of action. Given the external violation of a law, the evil will is presumed in the external forum until the contrary is proved."[81]

Let us look also at the practice of the Church. Let us say a man was baptized in the Anglican Church as an infant in a manner that we know is valid. He is raised in this church his whole life. He is reading something when he is thirty and realizes that the Catholic Church is the true Church of Jesus Christ. He presents himself to the Catholic pastor of his hometown. What will the pastor do? Will the pastor simply tell him to come to Church on Sunday and go to Mass and Communion? No, the Church requires he take the full convert course. At the end of this convert course he is required to make the Profession of Faith and be absolved from the excommunication for heresy. However, it is most likely he never committed the sin of heresy.

---

81 <u>A Practical Commentary On The Code Of Canon Law</u>, Volume 2, Canon 2200, Page: 450

Although Canon 2200 allows for contrary proof, I have never seen a case of heresy that has been adjudicated by the Church and been declared innocent on the grounds of ignorance. And to what court would we have to appeal? The only competent court to decide innocence is that of the Roman Pontiff. Canon Law, however, allows the Local Ordinary to absolve all who present their cases of heresy before him.

Basically, if a person doubts or denies a doctrine of the Faith publicly (that is, in the presence of six people), we must presume that he is heretic and have incurred all of the consequences of heresy.

Consequences

There are two main consequences of schism, heresy, and apostasy from which all of the others naturally flow. The first is complete departure from the Catholic Church without any need of declaration. From this naturally flows the loss of all authority in the Church a priest or bishop may have possessed. This is only reasonable. To depart from an organization is to lose any authority one may have had in that organization. Schism, heresy, and apostasy can be compared to the crime of treason. In the United States Constitution, treason is punishable by death. Schism, heresy, and apostasy are spiritual death. They are worse than mere mortal sin. Not only does one lose sanctifying grace, one cuts oneself off from the Church entirely.

The other consequence of schism - heresy and apostasy - is irregularity. Irregularity makes a man unfit to receive or exercise Holy Orders. This consequence is separate from the excommunication. In the case of the first consequence, by confession to the Local Ordinary, one can be absolved and return to the Church. After this juridical absolution in the name of the Church, the sin must be confessed. Once absolved in the confessional, one returns to sanctifying grace and can save his or her soul. However, once one has once been a schismatic, heretic, or an apostate, one is still unfit to receive or exercise Holy Orders. There are various things, whether physical or moral defects, which make one unfit for the Sacred Ministry. Read about the many regulations of the Old Testament in regard to the priesthood and the sacrifices. Would Jesus require less when His own Sacred Body and Blood are part of the Divine Liturgy?

Personally, I compare schism, apostasy, and heresy to a cesspool. No matter how one gets in the cesspool,[82] one thing is certain: he is dirty. If a person jumps into the cesspool he is dirty. If he falls into the cesspool he is dirty. If he is pushed into

---

82   A place where sewage is held. Example: sewage lagoon.

the cesspool he is still dirty. And this dirt remains on his soul until after he has bathed thoroughly. However, following the example of leprosy in the Old Testament, which is a symbol for heresy, it is not enough to clean oneself. One must be pronounced clean by the priests. Under the New Testament to return to the Faithful, Catholics must present themselves before the Local Bishop, that is the Local Ordinary or Diocesan Bishop as he is sometimes known, in order to return to the faithful. This is the practice in the case of adult converts who were validly baptized outside of the Church. However, to return to, or enter the clerical state, only the Pope can pronounce a person clean and free from the irregularity.

A Modern Heresy

> "In questions of faith also, the responsibilities of the Supreme Pontiff are principal ones, and his decrees pertain to all and individual churches, and yet this judgment is not unalterable unless the consent of the Church has been added to it."[83]

This heresy of the Gallicans[84] was condemned by Pope Alexander VIII. Yet, this is the attitude of many today. Instead **of Rome has spoken, the case is closed**, it is Rome has spoken, the debate is on. This position is now widely trumpeted by those who claim that Benedict XVI is Pope, while he says many things that are heretical, still has some claim to the papacy.

"The heresy which is now being born will become the most dangerous of all; the exaggeration of the respect due to the Pope and the illegitimate extension of his infallibility."[85] From these words it is argued that infallibility is extremely rare, and that the Pope is protected from heresy only when he defines something infallibly. There are two theories that are considered possible by theologians concerning whether or not a Pope can become a heretic. One theory is that this is impossible; the other theory admits that he might be able to become a heretic as

---

83   The Sources Of Catholic Dogma, # 1325, Page: 342

84   "The teaching set forth in a document called The Great Liberties, set out in four propositions drawn up by the clergy of the Church in France in 1682. The first proposition denied that Saint Peter and his successors received any power from God extending to temporal and civil affairs, declared princes to be subject to no ecclesiastical power in temporal matters, and denied the deposing power of the pope. The second declared the supremacy of ecumenical councils over the pope. The third affirmed the force and validity of the laws, customs, and constitutions of the Gallican and other local churches. The fourth declared that the pope has the principal share in questions of faith and that his decrees regard all the churches and every church in particular, but that his judgment is not irreformable unless the consent of the Church be added." (A Catholic Dictionary, Page: 205)

85   Fr. Le Floch was head of the French Seminary in 1926. This was addressed on page 22 as well.

a private person. His public acts, such as Encyclicals, are protected. However, he might be able to say something heretical in a sermon, or in a private conversation, or a private letter. Both schools of thought admit that a Pope has never committed an act of heresy, even as a private person.

Conclusion

Schism, heresy, or apostasy removes Catholics from the Church by their very word or deed. There is no need of any declaration on the part of the Church. This person loses all authority in the Catholic Church period. And I say to you: "Whosoever shall confess Me before men, him shall the Son of Man also confess before the angels of God. But he that shall deny Me before men shall be denied before the angels of God."[86] Saint Cyril comments on these verses: "Now they who deny are first indeed those who in time of persecution renounce the faith. Besides these, there are heretical teachers also, and their disciples."[87]

---

86   Luke 12:8-9
87   <u>Catena Aurea</u>, Saint Thomas Aquinas, Page: 435

Chapter 4
Passion of the Mystical Body of Christ

It is said that the Catholic Church, as the Mystical Body of Christ, will suffer a Passion similar to what Jesus suffered in His physical Body. There will be a time of intense persecution, the worst in history.[88] Scripture speaks of Antichrist, who will come at some time in history. Saint John Eudes states: "pray especially for those who will have to suffer the persecution of Antichrist at the end of the world, for it will be the most cruel and horrible of all persecutions,"[89] he tells us. But, he gives us hope: "All the holy Fathers agree that after the death of Antichrist the whole world will be converted."[90] There will be a time of intense persecution followed by a universal conversion.

Are we in these times? If not, I do not want to see times worse than these. However, even the Roman Catechism has apocalyptic references: "proportioned to the circumstances of the times in which we live, when men endure not sound doctrine."[91] Timothy 2:4 refers to the times of this persecution. Verse three is directly quoted by the Roman Catechism. One other thing should be noted. Saint Pius X in his first Encyclical[92] stated: "So extreme is the general perversion that there is room to fear...that the Son of Perdition, of whom the Apostle speaks, has already arrived on Earth."[93] The perversion is far worse today than in 1903 when Saint Pius X wrote these words. If he is right, then the Son of Perdition who is commonly held to be Antichrist is 120 years old, or has already come and gone.

---

88   Mark 13:19
89   The Life And The Kingdom Of Jesus In Christian Souls, Saint John Eudes, Page: 97
90   The Admirable Heart of Mary, Page: 319
91   Catechism of the Council of Trent, Page: 51
92   E Supremi Apostolatus, 4 October 1903
93   II Thessalonians 3:3. Antichrist is known by various names. Here Saint Paul calls him the man of sin and the Son of Perdition. Apocalypse 13 and parts of the book of Daniel also refer to Antichrist.

A Recurring Crisis

The Church has endured a crisis some 260 times throughout Her history, and we are in the middle of such a crisis now. The Church also has prepared for this crisis. She has provided numerous laws throughout the centuries to ensure that it will soon end. However, when this event happens, the Church is in yet another crisis. This event is the death of the Pope. When the Pope dies, the Church is instantly in mourning and prayer. We are directed by the laws of the Church to pray for a speedy and unanimous papal election. Normally, this crisis ends within a month and thus, this crisis causes little disruption in the Church. However, it does cause some disruption. The Apostolic See ceases to function until the new Pope has accepted election. In fact, the Popes issued new regulations in the Middle Ages because the Cardinals were found to be lax about completing the job of electing a Pope. One such crisis was met with the conclave law. The Cardinals gathered, but failed to complete an election for almost three years. The faithful considered this so severe that they locked the Cardinals up inside the place of conclave, boarding up the doors and windows. The faithful also restricted the Cardinals to bread and water until they completed their sacred task. When this did not accomplish the needed end to the crisis, the faithful took the roof off. The elements finally persuaded the cardinals to elect a pope. This crisis saw extraordinary actions taken to bring about its end. Also, some bishoprics became vacant. The law of the Church at that time required the Canons to elect a successor, and then present his name to the pope to be confirmed. After this, the bishop was then consecrated. However, there was no pope to send the name to, although an election was underway. Therefore, the Canons presumed papal permission, and proceeded to the consecration to ensure continuity in their diocese. The pope who was elected validated these appointments, although he could have set them aside. The Canons in question cannot be charged with willfully violating the law. They reached the conclusion that they should proceed with the consecration of the bishop for the good of the faithful. The need for a pastor in the diocese superseded the need for papal permission. This was certainly impossible to obtain.[94] The cardinals were at the root of many of the crises in the Papacy because they were slow to act and even fought against the conclave law.

The cardinals were to bring the Church to another crisis. They elected a pope, but claimed coercion. The cardinals proceeded to leave Rome and proceeded to elect another pope. This is called the Western Schism. Some sided with the second election while others sided with the first election. Eventually, cardinals appointed by claimants gathered in a council. They elected a third claimant to the papacy. This set both claims aside under the principle: **"a doubtful pope is no pope"**. Before continuing, let us note that none of the claimants were heretics. The claimants were all Catholics.

Saint Antonine of Florence stated:

> "Although it is necessary to believe that there is but one supreme head of the Church, nevertheless, if it happens that two popes are created at the same time, it is not necessary for the people to believe that this one or that one is the legitimate Pontiff; they must believe that he alone is the true pope who has been regularly elected, and they are not bound to discern who that one is; as to that point, they may be guided by the conduct and opinion of their particular pastor."[95]

Therefore, no one can be called a schismatic. All had to

---

[94] This does not provide any precedent for our time because none of the Traditionalist bishops consecrated have been consecrated to fill any vacant diocese. Therefore, they have no authority, and are not pastors in the Church.

[95] Studies in Church History, Volume 2, Page: 530

reach a conclusion as to which one of the two, (and eventually there were three papal claimants) was Pope, and then submit in obedience. Lay people followed their pastor, who followed his local Ordinary. The Ordinary made a decision based upon the laws of the Church at that time, and the opinions ventured by theologians and canonists. Note well everyone submitted to one of the claimants, because they realized it was necessary to have a living Pope and be in submission to him.

However, there had to be an end to the crisis. There cannot be three claimants to the papacy. However, this has to be handled properly. The first attempt at ending the crisis, the Council of Pisa, produced the third claimant to the papacy. It did not deal with the other two claimants, but merely set them aside. However, the Council of Constance first dealt with all of the claimants, then proceeded to fill the vacancy. The line coming from Pisa, which was now represented by John XXIII,[96] convened Constance. This Council proceeded to set him aside. He reluctantly acquiesced. Gregory XII, descending from Urban VI, resigned in favor of a new election to be held at Constance. The final line was set aside as invalid because it occurred subsequent to Urban VI. This being done, the cardinals from all three claimants, and twenty-five others assembled and elected Pope Martin V.

Pope Benedict XIV says: "today it is evident that Urban VI, and his successors were legitimate Pontiffs."[97] **This validates the tradition that the first in time is the first in right**. However, this theory was already on solid ground at the time of the Western Schism. As Honorious II lay dying, a few cardinals were very concerned over the machinations of Peter de Leone. And so, as soon as Honorious died, all six of these cardinals assembled. They immediately elected a Pope who took the name of Innocent II. In fact, it took longer to convince him to accept election than it did to elect him. After Innocent II

---

96   Not to be confused with Angelo Roncalli, who also took the name John XXIII in 1958.
97   Studies In Church History, Page: 539

accepted the election, they left town. Peter de Leone gathered the other cardinals and had himself elected pope by them. He took the name of Anacletus II. History, however, has always accepted Innocent II as the true pope. Peter de Leone's successor resigned in favor of Pope Innocent II. This confirms what Saint Alphonsus said later: "It matters little if in past centuries a given Pontiff was elected in an illegitimate fashion, or took possession of the pontificate by means of fraud: it suffices that he was subsequently accepted as Pope by the entire Church, because from this done, he becomes a true pontiff."[98]

It should be remembered that the Church by accepting a Pope into her official list of Popes has declared by this insertion that this is a dogmatic fact, and therefore, cannot be challenged by Catholics. It is a dogmatic fact, for instance, that Pope Innocent II was the true Pope, despite the fact that Anacletus II was elected by the majority of Cardinals. By inserting Innocent II into her official list of Popes, the Church has declared that the Pope first elected is the true Pope, because Innocent II was elected first by six Cardinals. Later Pope Benedict XIV would apply this same principle to declare that Pope Urban VI and his successors were the true Popes at the time of the Western Schism.

---

98   The Destruction of the Christian Tradition, Page: 119
      There wasn't any fraud, but a real concern by the Cardinals. Even fraud and simony will not invalidate an election, but they are serious sins. Only heresy invalidates an election.

Antipopes

Depending on the historian consulted, there are between forty and fifty antipopes from Saint Hippolytus in 217 to Felix V in 1449. Saint Hippolytus was reconciled with the true Pope as were many of the Antipopes throughout history. Antipopes usually sought the papacy for personal gain in opposition to a true Pope. Some antipopes had successors, who finally reconciled with the true pope, or whose line merely died out as do all human institutions.

Antipopes cause confusion among the faithful, because sometimes due to circumstances it is difficult to determine who the true Pope really is. The fact that a claimant lives in Rome is no proof that he is the Pope, if there is another claimant in Germany or France. There are now some simple principles that can be applied to determine whether or not a person is truly Pope or an usurping antipope. These are simple.

First of all, if there is a true Pope reigning, then anyone who launches a claim, whether from a council or a conclave or even an apparition in opposition to the true Pope is an antipope. Once a man accepts election as Pope, he becomes Pope, no matter how irregular the election may have been as tradition and history prove. Secondly it is certain that a heretic cannot become Pope, for a heretic is not a member of the Catholic Church and thus cannot become head of the Church. And this holds true even if the Papacy happens to be vacant, as Pope Paul IV infallibly declares in <u>Cum Ex Apostolatus Officio</u>.

The Crisis Begins

As with the previous crises, this one began simply with hope for an immediate end. Since there had been no problems in half a millennium, no one worried. The Church had not been plagued for half a millennium with an antipope. The papacy continued on, attacked, but solid. True, the Church had lost most of its possessions in Europe, but was able to function. On October 9, 1958, Pope Pius XII died. Thus, began the crisis. The crisis appeared to end rapidly just as the previous crises had. People did not have any concerns. However, things were not as they appeared.

In fact, there was confusion in the conclave that convened October 25, 1958. On October 26, 1958 white smoke went up. In fact, there are reports that the conclave was opened, as if a pope had been elected. However, reports soon circulated that there had been no election. There is much speculation about what happened that day. Some news reports stated that Cardinal Ottaviani, a cardinal deacon, had been elected Pope. Some more recent reports[99] indicated that Giuseppe Cardinal Siri, Archbishop of Genoa, had been elected pope. He was forced not to accept, thus, making him a Pope elect.[100] What truly happened on October 26 may never be known. However, the conclave continued until October 28 when it was announced that Angelo Roncalli had been elected as pope.

---

99 These reports were first circulated in the early 1990's, and have even spawned a book.
100 True, an action is not considered free if it is forced, but there is no precedent for a pope elect. One either accepts or rejects election. For instance, a man was questioned whether he accepted election or not. He replied: If it is God's will. The Cardinal merely repeated the question because acceptance must be clear and certain.

Angelo Roncalli

There are several serious questions about this man. Since this presentation is intended to be brief, it will rely on other evidence previously published, and merely summarized. First of all, this man took the name and number of a previous antipope, an action unprecedented in history.[101] This is interesting if one considers the report that Angelo Roncalli was John XXIII in two organizations: the Priory of Zion and the Catholic Church.[102] This would explain his taking a number already used by an antipope. It is also claimed that Roncalli was a member of the Rosicrucians, an apostate secret society.

In 1945, Roncalli gave a speech and stated:

> "We have come to pray for Christian Unity and we pray as Catholics; but in order to attain this particular aim we pray in union with our brothers who belong to other Christian confessions: Orthodox, Greek and Slav; Protestants of all shades, peoples of all nationalities and all languages who believe in Christ."[103]

This contradicts three heresies condemned by Pope Pius IX in the Syllabus.[104] As stated above, one heresy is sufficient to

---

101 John XXIII, as stated above. There was also an antipope John XXIII during the Western Schism. If an antipope had taken a name, and if the name was used again, the next number was taken to avoid confusion.
102 See the book, <u>Holy Blood, Holy Grail</u>. This is not an endorsement of this blasphemous book, but the information presented therein has never been contested. Therefore, can we presume silence gives consent?
103 <u>Mission To France</u>, Page: 8
104 Note the following propositions were condemned in the <u>Syllabus of Errors</u>:
    1. "Everyman is free to embrace and profess that religion, which he led by the light of reason, thinks to be the true religion." (DZ 1715)
    2. "In the worship of any religion whatever, men can find the way to eternal salvation, and can attain eternal

remove one from the Catholic Church. The cardinals in 1958 should have been aware of this. This was not an isolated incident, but one given here to demonstrate the thinking of this heresiarch. In a conclave, the electors vow to vote for the man they considered most qualified. Cardinals, especially, should know that heretics are not qualified at all![105]

The enactments coming out of Rome during his reign should have also given bishops pause to consider. There is not space here to consider everything Roncalli did while claiming to be Pope. However, he did order the insertion of Saint Joseph into the Canon of the Mass in 1962. **The Canon of the Mass had not been touched for over a millennium.** This should have given priests and bishops pause to consider, especially in light of an action by Pope Pius XII shortly before his death. On June 2, 1957, Pope Pius XII extended certain Canons of the Oriental Code of Canon Law to the Latin Church; including Canon 1, paragraph 2: "Patriarchs, Archbishops and other Ordinaries should zealously care for the faithful observance of their rite, nor are they to permit or to tolerate any change in the rite." Some may argue that the Pope is like the proverbial 800 pound gorilla.[106] The Pope can change the non-essential parts of the Mass and

---

       salvation." (DZ 1716)

3.   "Protestantism is nothing else that a different form of the same true Christian religion, in which it is possible to serve God as well as in the Catholic Church." (DZ 1718)

105   This also applies to Ottaviani and Siri who should have denounced Roncalli as a heretic. They should have called together the faithful Cardinals, even if it was only themselves, and then elected a Pope. This should have been done, no matter what violence was threatened against themselves or Catholics in general. The crisis would have been avoided if they had had the courage they should have had. Courage is represented by the red of their cassocks. This red indicates their willingness to give their lives for the Catholic Faith. Their cowardice gives one pause to wonder if they were ready to defect from the Catholic Faith themselves. Remember that all in the conclave know what happened there, and were responsibility bound to bring it to light for the good of the Church.

106   There is a story in America. Where does an 800 pound gorilla sleep? Anywhere he wants to.

Sacraments.¹⁰⁷ They can claim that the Pope was doing just this. However, this should have caused some concern.

What should have awakened all Catholics is the Encyclical, <u>Pacem in Terris</u>. This Encyclical restated many heresies previously condemned by the Church. This should have caused all, especially bishops, who are required to keep heresy out of their dioceses, to look into matters. However, <u>Pacem in Terris</u> was met with praise, not questions.

At this point, let us reach some conclusions. Canon Law states that if a college elects one unfit to hold an office, the electors disqualify themselves by that very act. By electing a heretic, the cardinals¹⁰⁸ all joined implicitly in his heresy. Thus, ceasing to be cardinals.¹⁰⁹ True, it would have taken time for the bishops to find out what had happened, but there were things coming from Rome that started almost from the beginning of Roncalli's usurpation of the papacy. And all should have become obvious at Vatican II.¹¹⁰ Since the cardinals had resigned, the 1963 conclave could not have been valid.¹¹¹ Also, since Roncalli

---

107 The Pope is not bound by Church Law, and is its author. Theoretically, he can change non-essential rites. However, this would be a novelty that Popes have fought for centuries. The 1983 Code of Canon Law states that the Pope writes the liturgy, apparently indicating he can change anything he wishes. Essential or non-essential.
108 And this includes all the participants, because by remaining silent, they consented to the election when Roncalli came on to the balcony. True, they may have had to wait a day or two until they could flee Rome, but they were responsibility bound to flee Rome and announce to the world that Roncalli was an antipope!
109 Canon 188, paragraph 4 states that those who publicly abandon the Faith resign from all offices within the Church, and the Church accepts their resignation without any need of further declaration. By presenting a man as Pope and knowing he was not, they publicly abandoned the Faith.
110 This will be discussed later. We can presume a priest or bishop became a material schismatic the day he inserted John XXIII's name in the Canon, and especially the first time he prayed publicly for the antipope because they were ignorant of the true facts. We can assume ignorance because this hadn't become obvious to them.
111 Also, Roncalli had appointed so many Cardinals. It was impossible to obtain the required two thirds plus one vote, without having votes from

was not pope, we can dismiss Vatican II because it was called by an antipope.[112]

> "There can be no Ecumenical Council unless it is convoked by the Roman Pontiff. It is the right of the Roman Pontiff to preside over the Ecumenical Council either in person or through others; to determine the matters to be discussed and in what order; to transfer, suspend, or dissolve the Council, and to confirm its decrees."[113]

Therefore, Roncalli, as an antipope, could not convoke a council for he was not in the Church as her proper head. His actions are ipso facto (by the very fact) null and void. All decrees promulgated at Vatican II, can be ignored, if not anathematized.

---

invalid Cardinals. It has also been demonstrated from Montini's own writings that he was also a heretic prior to his election. It is interesting to note that the early claims for Siri indicated he was elected for the first time in 1963. Only after <u>Will the Catholic Church Survive the Twentieth Century?</u> was published in 1990 was there proof that this conclave was invalid. Then there were claims he had been elected in 1958.

112   This would be true even if he was an antipope for some other reason. Although, an antipope called Constance, it was only considered valid after Pope Gregory XII convoked it, and resigned in favor of a new election there. Several decrees prior to that point were subsequently approved by Pope Martin V, while others were rejected by the same Pope.

113   <u>A Practical Commentary On The Code Of Canon Law</u>, Volume 1, Canon 222, Page: 99

Chapter 5
Vatican II

We can dismiss Vatican II as an heretical council, just like we dismiss the Synod of Pistoia.[114] However, since many of the bishops appear to have been unaware of the true situation when they arrived in Rome for Vatican II, we should consider a few points of this Council, as it is time to set aside some of the misconceptions. In several decrees preparing for Vatican II, it is called: "Second Ecumenical Council of the Vatican."[115] Those who claim that Vatican II was merely a pastoral council, and not an Ecumenical Council (considered by John XXIII, Paul VI, and the bishops participating to be on a par with Trent, the 1869-70 Vatican Council, and the other Ecumenical Councils) are absolutely wrong. The intention was to define Catholic doctrine in an apparently infallible manner. **A pastoral council is unheard of in the history of the Church.** True, in the past, particular councils have been called to resolve certain issues, or to declare the facts, as Pope Innocent II did in his time. However, this was called as a Universal and Ecumenical Council. Therefore, if a Pope had called it, it would have defined doctrine. However, we have already seen that Angelo Roncalli was not Pope, but a heretical antipope. Therefore, Vatican II was not Catholic.

It is interesting to note that in his memoirs, <u>Milestones</u>, Joseph Ratzinger commented:

---

114 This was held by the Jansenists to define their doctrines. It was condemned in the Bull <u>Auctorem Fidei</u>, DZ 1501ff. It is interesting to note that many of the heresies condemned in <u>Auctorem Fidei</u> have risen again.

115 <u>Canon Law Digest</u>, Page: 239 & 243

This Council was first announced on January 25, 1959. "We institute, announce, and convoke for the forthcoming year 1962 the Ecumenical and Universal Council, which will be held in the Vatican Basilica,...Given at Rome at Saint Peter's, December 25, feast of the birth of our Lord Jesus Christ, 1961, fourth year of Our Pontificate, I John, Bishop of the Catholic Church." (From <u>Documents of Vatican II</u>, Pages: 708-709. Montini as Antipope Paul VI would sign all the documents: "I Paul, Bishop of the Catholic Church.").

"For believers, it was a remarkable phenomenon that their bishops seemed to show a different face in Rome from the one they wore at home. Shepherds who had been considered strict conservatives suddenly appeared to be spokesmen for progressivism."[116]

---

[116] www.losangelesmission.com/ed/articles/2000/0400cr.htm

The First Heretical Document

When heretics assemble, as they have throughout history, they assemble to give their heresies the appearance of Catholicity. "He who deserts the Church will vainly believe that he is in the Church."[117] Many heresies can be found in Vatican II documents. Heresies cannot be interpreted in a good light no matter how you read them. The Decree on the Liturgy stands out because it was approved on a vote of 2,174 to 4.[118] In fact, in a subsequent decree to begin the project set forth in this document, Montini said "this document was approved almost unanimously by the Second Ecumenical Council of the Vatican, and [which We] promulgated in solemn session on 4 December, 1963."[119] Therefore, if this document is found to be heretical, then we must immediately conclude that by voting for it; 2,174 bishops immediately departed from the Catholic Church then if they had not already done so before their vote.

Pope Saint Pius X said:

> "First of all they," (the Modernists) "lay down the general principle that in a living religion everything is subject to change, and must in fact change, and in this way they pass to what may be said to be among the chief of their doctrines, that of Evolution. To the doctrine of evolution, everything is subject to change, dogma, Church worship, the Books we revere as sacred, even faith itself, and the penalty of disobedience is death."[120]

---

117   Saint Cyprian, quoted in Amantissimus, Pope Pius IX, Paragraph 3
118   It is unknown whether or not the four dissenters eventually signed the document or not.
119   Here is a reference to Antipope Paul VI attempting to use infallibility. The Catholic Church considers the decrees of Council are infallible when they are approved by the Pope.
120   Pascendi, Pope Saint Pius X, Paragraph 26

Vatican II teaches:

> "For the liturgy is made up of unchangeable elements divinely instituted, and of elements subject to change. These latter not only may be changed, but ought to be changed with the passage of time, if they have suffered from the intrusion of anything out of harmony with the inner nature of the liturgy or have become less suitable."[121]

The decree in question, one of the first approved by the Second Ecumenical Council of the Vatican (ie Vatican II), is: Sacrosanctum Concilium. This decree was promulgated by Paul VI on December 4, 1963. But one can immediately see that what is contained in this decree is the heresy of Modernism. And so, can this be Catholic doctrine? Absolutely not! However, the solution is simple. Giovanni Baptiste Montini never became pope in the first place. Never in history has an antipope been succeeded by a true pope. We have already demonstrated that Angelo Roncalli, who called the Second Ecumenical Council of the Vatican and appointed Montini as cardinal, was an antipope. Since Montini was an antipope, none of his actions while usurping the papacy have any validity whatsoever.

Now the bishops are required by divine law to know the Catholic faith. The bishops under the pope form the Ecclesia Docens or Teaching Church. Divine law requires them not only to know the Faith and teach it untainted to their flocks, but also to root out and expose heretics. For this reason, Saint Paul wrote to Saint Titus about heretics.[122] Canon Law gives local ordinaries[123] the authority to absolve any heretics whose heresy

---

121 Vatican Council II: The Conciliar and Post Conciliar Documents, Page: 9

122 "A man that is a heretic, after the first and second admonition, avoid. Knowing that he, that is such an one, is subverted, and sinneth, being condemned by his own judgment." (Titus 3:10-11)

123 "A cleric with ordinary jurisdiction in the external forum over a speciified territory. The following are local ordinaries: the pope universally,

has become public in their diocese, when they ask for absolution from excommunication.[124] The bishops at Vatican II had a book with them called Henry Denzinger's <u>Enchiridion Symbolorum</u>. This book contains many infallibly true decrees from the Church, the popes, and from Councils approved by the popes.[125] Further, these bishops had taken the Antimodernist Oath on four occasions.[126] They should have read <u>Pascendi</u> on several occasions to remind themselves of the heresy of Modernism these bishops were bound to fight with all of their might.

Let us read from the Decree on the Liturgy of Vatican II:

> "As regards to the readings (in the Divine Office), the following points shall be observed: Readings from sacred scripture shall be so arranged that the riches of the divine word may be easily accessible in more abundant measure; Readings taken from the works of the fathers, doctors, and ecclesiastical writers shall be better selected; The accounts of the martyrdom or lives of the saints are to be made historically accurate. Hymns are to be restored to their original form, as far as may be desirable. They are to be purged of whatever smacks of mythology or accords ill with Christian

---

residential bishops in their dioceses, abbots and prelates-nullius, vicars general, administrators, vicars and prefects apostolic, vicars capitular. The expression the ordinary generally indicates the bishop of the diocese." (<u>A Catholic Dictionary</u>, Page: 358)

124 However, a Bishop cannot remove the irregularity which is reserved exclusively to the Pope.

125 We have already referred to Denzinger's, and refer to the 30th edition, which is in English translation as <u>The Sources of Catholic Dogma</u>. However, some significant decrees have been omitted from this work, and a newer, larger work (in Latin only) was available to the Bishops at Vatican II.

126 Pope Saint Pius X required this oath prior to ordination to each major order. That is: the subdiaconate, diaconate, and priesthood, as well as before the consecration as Bishop, when the Profession of Faith of the Council of Trent, as amended by the only Vatican Council, must also be made.

piety..."[127]

These bishops should have been aware of the changes already underway prior to this decree, as it states:

> "In order that the divine office may be better and more perfectly prayed, whether by priests or by other members of the Church, in existing circumstances, the sacred Council, continuing the restoration so happily begun by the Apostolic See, decrees..."[128]

Before going into the changes made in the Divine Office, it should be noted that the Sacred Canon of the Mass has been untouched for well over a millennium. Until the insertion of Saint Joseph into the Canon of the Mass in 1962. This is the so-called 1962 Missal. It cannot claim to be the Tridentine Mass because of this substantial change. <u>Quo Primum</u> was quite specific in forbidding any change. This was renewed by Pope Pius XII.[129]

On July 25, 1960, Antipope John XXIII issued <u>Rubricarum Instructum</u> to amend the Universal Calendar of the Church. This of itself is not unusual because Pope Saint Pius X had amended the calendar and breviary. Pope Pius XII had also amended the calendar and breviary. However, this change had the spirit of Modernism. First of all, several feasts of the Blessed Virgin Mary were reduced to optional commemorations.[130] Also,

---

127   <u>Vatican Council II: The Conciliar and Post Conciliar Documents</u>, Page: 26
128   <u>Vatican Council II: The Conciliar and Post Conciliar Documents</u>, Page: 25
129   <u>The Canon Law Digest</u>, volume 5, Page: 7 by motuproprio dated June 2, 1957.
130   "I am worried by the Blessed Virgin's message to Lucia of Fatima. This persistence of Mary about dangers which menace the Church is a divine warning against the suicide of altering the faith in her history, her theology, and her soul...I hear all around me innovators who wish to dismantle the

the most significant omission is that of Saint Peter's Chair at Rome on January 18th. Was Roncalli telling us in an underhanded way that he had usurped, and was attempting to destroy this chair? The most significant trend is established by a supplementary decree on amending particular calendars to conform with <u>Rubricarum Instructum</u>.[131] "Let it be a general principle that a Saint or Mystery is to have but one feast."[132] And further on a whole list of feasts is ordered expunged (i.e. removed) from such calendars, including many of the Blessed Virgin Mary.[133] Also notable is a specific mention of Saint Philomena.

Speaking of the Modernists, Pope Saint Pius X says:

"Regarding worship, the number of external devotions is to be reduced, or at least steps must be taken to prevent their further increase, though, indeed some of the admirers of symbolism are disposed to be more indulgent on this head."[134]

It can easily be seen by a look at the Vatican II calendar that little remains of the Catholic Calendar. With few exceptions, many feasts have been removed entirely, and of those that remain, many have been relocated.

"By recalling it" (the liturgy) "to a greater simplicity of rites, by expressing it in the vernacular language, by uttering it

---

Sacred Chapel, destroy the universal flame of the Church, reject her ornaments, and make her feel remorse for her historical past." (<u>Pie XII Devant L'Histoire</u>. Page: 52)

131   <u>The Canon Law Digest</u>, Page: 136

132   Instruction for the Revision of Particular Calendars and the Propers of Offices and Masses According to the Code of Rubrics, Sacred Congregation of Rites, 14 February 1961, Paragraph 11, <u>The Canon Law Digest</u>, Page: 136

133   Instruction for the Revision of Particular Calendars and the Propers of Offices and Masses According to the Code of Rubrics, Sacred Congregation of Rites, 14 February 1961, Paragraph 34, <u>The Canon Law Digest</u>, Page: 136

134   <u>Pascendi</u> condemned this proposition of the Modernists.

in a loud voice."[135] No this is not from Vatican II, but from the Jansenist Synod of Pistoia. Although, Vatican II decrees:

> "The rites should be distinguished by a noble simplicity. They should be short, clear, and free from useless repetitions. They should be within the people's powers of comprehension, and normally should not require much explanation."[136]

And further:

> "The rite of the Mass is to be revised in such a way that the intrinsic nature and purpose of its several parts, as well as the connection between them, may be more clearly manifested, and that devout active participation by the faithful may be more easily achieved. For this purpose the rites are to be simplified, due care being taken to preserve their substance. Parts which with the passage of time came to be duplicated, or were added with little advantage, are to be omitted. Others parts which suffered loss through accidents of history are to be restored to the vigor they had in the days of the holy Fathers, as may seem useful or necessary."[137]

Remember that this rite which is being declared contain things of little advantage, and had been in use unchanged for well over five centuries. Although Vatican II does not call for sole use of the vernacular, it does pave the way for it. Finally, in a simple look at the final edition of the

---

135   The Sources Of Catholic Dogma, # 1533, Page: 380
136   Vatican Council II: The Conciliar and Post Conciliar Documents, Page: 12
137   Vatican Council II: The Conciliar and Post Conciliar Documents, Page: 17

reformed liturgy, we will see that all three requirements[138] of the heretical Jansenists have been met.

Ecumenism, which would become prominent later on in Vatican II is to be seen in the last part of this decree on the proposal of a universal calendar. This would place Easter on a fixed Sunday of the year.[139]

> "It (Second Ecumenical Council of the Vatican) would not object if the feast of Easter were assigned to a particular Sunday of the Gregorian Calendar, provided that those whom it may concern give their consent, especially the brethren who are not in communion with the Apostolic See."[140]

One last item needs to be discussed. "It is fitting that the use of pontificals be reserved to those ecclesiastical persons who have the episcopal rank or some particular jurisdiction."[141] Pontificals are the miter, crosier, pectoral cross, and other symbols that are given to bishops. By long custom, pontificals have been extended to abbots and other priests. The honorary title Monsignor; conferred by the pope on some priests, sometimes also comes with the right to use the miter, and usually to wear the mantelletta over the rochet, instead of the usual plain surplice. Vicars General also have the right to

---

138   1) A greater simplicity of rites.
      2) By expressing it in the vernacular language.
      3) By uttering it in a loud voice.
139   This proposal was circulating in the secular world at that time, and a small minority are still working for such a calendar today. The main proposal is to fix January 1 as a Sunday, and all of the other days of the year to a specific day of the week. At the end of the year, a day outside of the week would be added, or two in leap years, to preserve the order. Various ways of formatting the months have been proposed.
140   The Documents of Vatican II, Page: 177
141   Vatican Council II: The Conciliar and Post Conciliar Documents, Page: 36

pontificals from their office. However, Vatican II is preparing to reserve pontificals to bishops and abbots alone. This is to further the new doctrine: that authority in the Church is conferred by episcopal consecration and abbatial blessing, not by Apostolic appointment. This false doctrine was extended when Antipope Paul VI decreed that a man does not receive his authority as Pope until he is consecrated bishop. This denies almost two millennia of tradition to the contrary.[142] This was further extended to all bishops in the Vatican II Church's Code of Canon Law issued in 1983. This revised law does not grant a man authority as a diocesan bishop until he has been consecrated bishop, although an apostolic appointment is also required.[143]

Let us consider one final quote from the Decree on the Liturgy: "For the liturgy is made up of unchangeable elements divinely instituted, and of elements subject to change."

---

[142] When Jesus appointed Peter, he was not yet ordained. It was nearly a millennium until the man elected Pope was bishop prior to his election. The coronation originated from the consecration of the Pope as Bishop. The last man before Vatican II to be elected Pope, who was not already a Bishop, was Pope Gregory XVI in the early 19th century.

[143] I saw part of a consecration of bishops by Karol Wojtyla. They did not even receive the customary zucchetto as a bishop until after the laying on of hands by Wojtyla. Confirming this new doctrine.

What Are the Consequences of This?

Many of the consequences have been enumerated above, but a brief review is in order. First of all, not only does this affect the 2,174 bishops who voted for the <u>Decree on the Liturgy</u>, but also the four bishops who voted against it. These four bishops were affected because they did not immediately sound the alarm about the heresies contained in the Decree. Among this number are those valiant defenders of Tradition. They are: Archbishops Lefebvre and Ngo-Dihn Thuc, and Bishops de Castro Meyer, Pintonello, and Mendez. Lefebvre admits to signing this document. He must have found nothing wrong with the Novus Ordo at first because he celebrated it until Christmas Eve, 1971.[144] There is not any information on whether or not Ngo-Dihn Thuc, de Castro Meyer, or Pintonello signed the <u>Decree on the Liturgy</u>. Ngo-Dihn Thuc also celebrated the Novus Ordo, although it is probable de Castro Meyer did not. However, all 2,179 bishops who were present became public heretics. Therefore, these bishops departed from the Catholic Church by their own judgment without any need of their declaration. Further, they tendered their resignation by their vote and/or signature. The Church accepted their resignation by operation of Her law.[145] This caused the majority of episcopal Sees in the world to become vacant as the papacy had been for five years. Further, these men were now forbidden by the Catholic Church from administering the Sacraments under any circumstances whatsoever, until a true pope could remove that prohibition.[146]

We can safely, but sadly report, that on or before December 4, 1963, the hierarchy defected from the Divine and

---

144 The SSPX gives the date now as 10 June 1971.
145 <u>A Practical Commentary On The Code Of Canon Law</u>, Volume 1, Canon 188, Page: 86
146 These are the two irregularities which were mentioned above. The Church gives no exception in Canon Law for the irregular, **even in danger of death**. Although, one might interpret Canon 882 to grant them authority to absolve someone in the confessional when that person is in danger of death. We have found no decisions in this matter.

Catholic Faith. The hierarchy conspired with Giovanni Baptiste Montini, beginning the deception of the elect foretold in Sacred Scripture.[147] The only exceptions are those bishops who were not present at Vatican II and have not given subsequent consent to any of its heretical decrees or pledged obedience to any of the antipopes reigning for the past 52 years.

---

147   Matthew 24:24

What of Their Progeny?

Bishops returning to their dioceses after tacit resignation usurped their sees and ordained men to the priesthood. A few others began ordaining men for the Traditionalist Church after the introduction of the Novus Ordo. The Traditionalist Church was founded to preserve the Latin Mass[148] and traditional devotions.

"All persons who presume to receive orders from a prelate who...is a notorious apostate, heretic, or schismatic[149] automatically incur suspension **a divinis**[150] reserved to the Apostolic See."[151] The word presume means to knowingly receive orders from such a man. This Canon continues: "Any person who has been ordained in good faith by such men, forfeits the right to exercise the order thus received until he obtains dispensation from the prohibition."[152] All ordained in this manner are forbidden to exercise their orders, until the Pope remove this prohibition. The reason is simple. There must be an investigation made into the ordination to see if it was even valid. However, this proven, the man was probably not properly trained and canonically fit. This must be remedied. The Apostolic See will determine exactly what must be done before this man is allowed to administer the Sacraments.

---

148   This has never really been defined by Traditionalists. Some accept the changes of Roncalli and Rubricarum Instructum. Some even accept the addition of Saint Joseph to the Canon and the 1962 Missal. While the last group rejects everything from 1950 on.

149   These bishops are notorious schismatics for accepting a heretic as their Pope. They are heretics for signing this heretical document as many others were at Vatican II.

150   "Suspension **a divinis** forbids the exercise of every act of the power of orders which hone obtained either by sacred orders or by privilege." (A Practical Commentary On The Code Of Canon Law, Volume 2, Canon 2279, Page: 496)

151   A Practical Commentary On The Code Of Canon Law, Volume 2, Canon 2372, Page: 559

152   A Practical Commentary On The Code Of Canon Law, Volume 2, Canon 2372, Page: 559

Is Allah God?

Vatican II states:

"The Church regards with esteem also the Moslems. **They adore the one God, living and subsisting in Himself;** merciful and all-powerful, the Creator of Heaven and Earth,[153] who has spoken to men; they take pains to submit wholeheartedly to even His inscrutable decrees, just as Abraham, with whom the faith of Islam takes pleasure in linking itself, submitted to God. Though they do not acknowledge Jesus as God, they revere Him as a prophet. They also honor Mary, His virgin Mother; at times they even call on her with devotion. In addition, they await the day of judgment when God will render their deserts to all those who have been raised up from the dead. Finally, they value the moral life and worship God especially through prayer, almsgiving and fasting. Since in the course of centuries not a few quarrels and hostilities have arisen between Christians and Moslems, this sacred synod urges all to forget the past and to work sincerely for mutual understanding and to preserve as well as to promote together for the benefit of all mankind social justice and moral welfare, as well as peace and freedom."[154]

Vatican II states that the Moslems worship the one true God. There is much talk of the three great monotheistic

---

153 Footnote from the original decree of Vatican II. Cf Saint Gregory VII, letter XXI to Anzir (Nacir), King of Mauritania (Pl. 148, col. 450f.) (Editor's note, we have reproduced the entire letter at the end of this book.)
154 Vatican Council II: The Conciliar and Post Conciliar Documents, Page: 740

religions, Judaism, Christianity and Islam. And yet, do these three religions worship the same God? Let us consider two people, who are monotheists, but worship different gods. There are three possibilities. The first person worships the true God, while the second does not. The second person worships the true God, while the first does not. Finally, both could be worshiping false gods. It is impossible for two people to worship different gods and both worship the true God.

Let us apply this principle to the statement above. By stating that Moslems worship the one true God, Vatican II is stating one of two things. Either they are stating that by worshiping a different god, Vatican II does not worship the one true God, or they are stating that the Islamic god, Allah is the one true God. Vatican II states that Islam rejects the Divinity of our Lord Jesus Christ, yet attempts to minimize this. This raises the question, "Who is the god of Vatican II?"

Are the New Rites of the Sacraments Valid?

Let us consider one final quote from the <u>Decree on the Liturgy</u>: "For the liturgy is made up of unchangeable elements divinely instituted, and of elements subject to change." In light of this decree, one would presume that the New Rites of the Sacraments promulgated by Paul VI in the late 1960's and early 1970's must be valid.

Many claim, however, that the Rites of the Sacraments are substantially different than the Catholic Rites. Let us consider this proposition for a moment.

The Rite of Baptism remains substantially the same, although some are not zealous about making sure the water flows on the head of the person being baptized, and this includes John Paul II and Benedict XVI, as pictures on the internet demonstrate. Also the accidental Rites are not clear about the purpose of Baptism until about 1990, when they were revised to express the Catholic doctrine of Baptism in regard to the removal of Original Sin, which has been omitted from the original New Rite of Baptism.

The Rites of the other Sacraments, though, have been changed, as we shall see.

N, I sign thee with the sign of N, be sealed with the Gift of the Cross, and I confirm you the Holy Spirit.[156]
with the Chrism of salvation in
the name of the Father, and of
the Son, and of the Holy
Ghost.[155]

Above are the essential Rite of Confirmation, the Catholic on the left and the New Rite on the right.

---

155   <u>The Roman Ritual</u>, Page: 53
156   <u>The Rites of the Catholic Church</u>, Page: 223

Through the holy anointing and His most tender mercy, may the Lord forgive you whatever you have committed by the sense of (sight, hearing, etc.).[157]	Through this holy anointing may the Lord in his love and mercy help you with the grace of the Holy Spirit. May the Lord who frees you from sin save you and raise you up.[158]

The Sacrament of Extreme Unction has been renamed as Anointing of the Sick. The Rite of Catholic Extreme Unction is on the left and the Rite of Anointing of the Sick on the right.

Fill up in Thy priest the perfection of Thy ministry, and sanctify him with the dew of Thy heavenly ornaments of all beauty.[159]	So now pour out upon this chosen one that power which is from you the governing spirit when you gave to your beloved Son, Jesus Christ, the Spirit given by him to the holy apostles, who founded the Church in every place to be your temple for the unceasing glory and praise of your name.[160]

Above are reproduced the essential form from <u>Sacramentum Ordinis</u> of Pope Pius XII for the consecration of a Bishop, and the essential form of the New Rite of consecration of a Bishop, promulgated in 1968. There has been much discussion whether or not the New Rite of Ordination of priests and bishops is valid or not. When asked, Archbishop Lefebvre said the New Rite was valid, because it is Eastern Rite. More recently someone did research and determined that the New Rite of

---

157   <u>The Roman Ritual</u>, Page: 221
158   <u>The Rites of the Catholic Church</u>, Page: 319
159   <u>The Roman Ritual</u>, Pages: 339-340
160   <u>The Rites of the Catholic Church</u>, Page: 603

consecration of Bishops is indeed taken from the Eastern Rite ceremony of installation of a Patriarch. He concluded it is invalid, because the man being installed has already been consecrated a bishop previously. In the Catholic Rite, a man is consecrated bishop by three bishops, who all impose their hands and recite the form of consecration with the intention of consecrating. In the event the principle consecrator would not be a valid bishop or have the proper intention, the other two would supply. In the New Rite only the principle consecrator recites the form, while all of the bishops present impose their hands silently.

> "The liturgical reform which has been carried out in accordance with the Constitution of the Second Vatican Council has made certain changes in the essential formulae of the sacramental rites." [161]

In 1974 Antipope Paul VI issued a decree on the proper translation of the translation of the New Rites of the Sacraments. Note that he declares that the essential formulae have been modified. Therefore, when we see words that appear to be substantially different from the Catholic Rites, we must presume in light of this decree that they are substantially different and therefore invalid. This decree supersedes not only the Council of Trent, but Vatican II, which we considered above, which declared: "For the liturgy is made up of unchangeable elements divinely instituted, and of elements subject to change."

Fr. Berry in his commentary on the Apocalypse[162] states:

> "The followers of Antichrist will be marked with a character in imitation of the sign that St. John saw upon the foreheads of the servants of God. This

---

161   Vatican Council II: The Conciliar and Post Conciliar Documents, Page: 271
162   The Apocalypse of St. John, Fr. E. Sylvester Berry, Page: 138

indicates that Antichrist and his prophet will introduce ceremonies to imitate the Sacraments of the Church."

We could conclude that Paul VI, by substantially changing the Catholic Sacraments has introduced imitation Sacraments and therefore he is the Antichrist. We must conclude that he intended the New Rites to be substantially different from the Catholic Rites, for he has declared this is his intention in an official decree.

The Novus Ordo Missae

"Joseph Gelineau, S.J. one of the members of Archbishop Bugnini's Consilium that composed the new Novus Ordo service, spoke of the Roman liturgy saying, '...the Roman Rite as we knew it no longer exists. It has been destroyed.' Msgr. Bugnini himself declared, 'The liturgical reform is a major conquest of the Catholic Church.'" [163]

In the Mass itself, substantial changes were made. The offertory, which is considered essential by many theologians, was totally changed. The **chalice of salvation** has become the **work of human hands**. The consecration of the bread into the Body of Christ has also been substantially changed by the addition of the words: **which was given up for you.** The Council of Trent issued a decree called De Defectibus to be added to the Roman Missal. It states: "Any substantial change, addition, or omission in the consecration form invalidates the form." This applies especially to the consecration of the wine. Two changes were made. The first appears apparently only in the vernacular. The words **pro multis** in the Latin are translated into the vernacular of every language that we have consulted as: **for all**. Obviously, many does not mean all. If I say many people support me, then you know that some do not, whereas; if I say all, then you know that these people are unanimous in their support.

Beginning in 2008 a move was made to correct this mistranslation of the words **pro multis** and have become effective in many parts of the world and will soon be effective world-wide. Also some places correctly translated the words **pro multis**, to **for many**, such as Poland as was recently discovered. However, this does not settle the issue, as will be soon seen. Recall that many who will now use the correct form,

---

[163] www.fatimainquiry.blogspot.com/

have been ordained in an Ordination Rite that is not Catholic and thus are not priests. Further, the bishop that ordained them may not be a valid bishop.

Antipope Paul VI, in his decree <u>Missale Romanum</u>[164] gives the consecration form to use. Over the bread: "Take this, all of you, and eat it; this is my body which will be given up for you." Over the wine: "Take this, all of you, and drink from it; this is the cup of my blood, the blood of the new and everlasting covenant. It will be shed for you and for all men so that **sins may be forgiven**. Do this in memory of me." The words, "The mystery of faith," spoken by the priest are to be taken out of the context of the words spoken by our Lord, and used instead to introduce an acclamation by the faithful.

Before continuing, the official Latin text at the Vatican website[165] contains **pro multis**, the official translation into Italian, and at the same website can also be found **per tutti** which means: **for all**.[166] This indicates that when they say **pro multis** in Latin, they intend, **for all**, despite the fact of using different words. This perverse intention alone is heretical and invalid.

We should expand. In 1970 questions were sent to Rome on this substantial change in many vernacular translations.[167] Rome answered with a Notitiae (Number 50) [168] in January of 1970:

---

164   Vatican Council II: The Conciliar and Post Conciliar Documents, Page: 139
165   www.vatican.va
166   Unlike many other documents, there is not an official English translation at this website. The others on the internet revert to Latin for the actual form, although attendance at a Novus Ordo service will instantly indicate which form is truly in use.
167   This substantial change occurs in English, German, Italian, French and Spanish. However, this author has recently learned, that Polish retains for many, being an exact translation of the Latin pro multis.
168   The complete text of the Notitiae is reproduced at the end of this book, as well as the Catholic teaching from the Roman Catechism.

"In some vernacular versions the words of the formula for the consecration of the wine **pro multis**'are translated in the following way: in English **for all men**; in Spanish **por todos** and in Italian **per tutti**. Is there a good reason, and if there is, what is it, for deciding on such a variation? Rome answered: The above variation is fully justified: a) According to exegetes, the Aramaic word which in Latin is translated **pro multis**, means **pro omnibus**: the multitude for whom Christ died is unbounded, which is the same as saying: Christ died for all."

More questions were sent in May of 1970 a much longer Notitiae was issued to confirm this new meaning. In concludes: "It is clear how the Church of the Apostles was not interested in preserving the very voice of the Lord even in the words of the consecration, certainly cited for the first time as such by Jesus himself."[169] In fact, this whole document is a Modernist jumble of contorted reasoning to imply that Jesus meant to say for all, but this was changed by the Apostles to for many, and only now we are changing it back. What are we to think? Were the Masses said from the time of the Apostles until the institution of the Novus Ordo invalid? In fact, is the Latin Novus Ordo invalid? Because it retains the incorrect **pro multis** form?

It should be remembered at the time, a theory was being circulated that Aramaic had no word for all. This was based upon the reasoning of a Protestant Theologian, who was the inspiration for this radical change. Confronted with this reasoning, a priest decided to check things out. He first visited a Jewish Aramaic scholar who told him that there is not one word for all, but six words that have this connotation. So this priest then went to see a Cardinal in Rome. He asked the Cardinal: "When Paul VI says Mass in Italian what does he say?" The Cardinal replied: "Per tutti." Which means "for all". The priest

---

169   www.zenit.org/english/visualizza.phtml?sid=58517

then asked: "And when he says Mass in Latin, what does he say?" The Cardinal replied: "pro multis", which means "for many." The priest then told the Cardinal that until Paul VI could figure it out, he was returning to the Tridentine Mass he was certain was valid.

And let us consider another point. Let us say that the Catholic Church has been wrong for almost two millennia in reporting Jesus' words as contained in the Gospels.[170] When the Protestants revolted in the Sixteenth Century, why didn't they discover this and call us to task for this? In fact, why haven't they corrected their Bibles to this very day, when one of their own has discovered this **Great Mistake**? Why did Paul VI personally approve the New American Bible for use by members of his church, which contains for many in both Gospel texts? He gave this approval on September 18, 1970, shortly after the two notices above. Since such things come across his desk, wouldn't he have some make sure the bible conforms to his new doctrine? There are many unanswered questions here. It is better to believe that the original reports from the Apostles, preserved unchanged for two millennia, not only by Catholics, but also by non-Catholics, are correct. In fact, the New Latin Vulgate on the Vatican website also contains pro multis in the pertinent passages.

Another notable change is to be found in even the Latin, that is the memorial acclamation ordered by Missale Romanum. "Christ has died, Christ has risen, Christ will come again." Wait a minute. Isn't Christ supposed to have come onto the very altar at the consecration? By reciting these words, the priest and people deny this. The priest has this denial in mind prior to the very mass[171] itself. Therefore, his intention cannot be valid. The addition of this memorial acclamation invalidates the whole service if nothing else does, and many other things do. **Therefore, we must conclude that celebrating the Novus**

---

170   Matthew 26:28 and Mark 14:24
171   I do not capitalize here because we are now certain that this service is not even really a Mass.

Ordo Missae is a heretical act, as well as not being a valid Mass. It is heretical to celebrate a Sacrament with an invalid rite. This disdains the rites of the Church.

The result of this is that any priest or bishop who celebrated the Novus Ordo Missae became a heretic ipso facto,[172] (if he wasn't one already), and incurred all of the same consequences enumerated for the bishops above.

---

172   By the very fact.

Surely This Cannot Be True

This may sound absurd, even impossible. Remember: The Jewish sacrifices were abrogated when Jesus died on the Cross and the Temple curtain was rent.[173] However, for almost 40 years the sacrifices continued in the Temple until shortly before it was destroyed in 70 AD. For this was a prefigure of the Novus Ordo and even valid but illegitimate masses offered to the devil. Let us look at Catholic History from <u>An Outline History of the Church</u> by Joseph McSorley:

> "Schism of 1054: This was the tragic outcome of numerous and ancient differences between the Greek Church and the Holy See. Michael Caerularius, Patriarch of Constantinople, without raising any strictly theological issue, built up a quarrel with the Pope out of protests against the eating of things strangled, the custom of fasting on Saturdays, the omission of the Alleluia during Lent, the use of unleavened bread for the Eucharist, and many other Latin practices. In all there were thirty-three distinct objections. On the strength of these, he decreed the closing of the Latin churches in Constantinople. Pope Leo IX sent Cardinal Frederick, the Future Stephen IX (X),[174] and Cardinal Humbert to negotiate with Caerularius. Their efforts were ineffective. On July 16, 1054, they entered the Church of Santa Sophia as service was about to begin. Laying upon the altar a papal bull excommunicating Caerularius and two Eastern bishops. Michael, in turn, excommunicated the Pope. Thereafter, the Church of Constantinople with the other Oriental Churches formed a group

---

173   Matthew 27:51
174   There was a discrepancy of the numbering of the Popes named Stephen.

known as the "Orthodox Eastern Church," in which the patriarchate of Constantinople possessed a certain precedence. The only Orientals retaining communion with Rome were the Byzantine Greeks in Italy, and the Maronites in Syria. As a result of the Greco-Latin break, the East was cut off from the guidance and protection of the papacy, and from the developing Christianity of the West. Latin Christianity was deprived of all those rich contributions which might have come from the Orientals and the Russians."[175]

Although these people started out by going into schism, part of them also fell later on into heresy. The Eastern Orthodox retained the Rites of the Mass. The Sacraments were unchanged, and the Eastern Orthodox Catholic retained the doctrine on these and their Mass. The Sacraments are considered valid, but Catholics are forbidden to receive the Sacraments from the Eastern Orthodox because they are at least schismatics. Let us return to this book:

> "Near the beginning of the Period, that is, soon after 1500, "The Protestant Revolt" broke out. Within a short time, a new religion aided by aggressive propaganda and armed force drew a large part of Germany and Northern Europe away from the Catholic communion. Thirty years later a reform program was adopted by the Council of Trent and put into operation by Pope Pius IV. The Church regained most of the lost area. By the end of the century, Western Christendom included two irreconcilable religious bodies...one-half of Europe having repudiated the authority of the pope, and other essential dogmas inherited from apostolic

---

175 An Outline History of the Church, Pages: 318-319

times."[176]

The first attack produced the Orthodox. The Orthodox merely repudiated the authority of the Pope, but the second attack added the heresy of personal infallibility. This personal infallibility makes each individual his very own pope. He decides for himself which doctrines and practices to accept and reject. The next attack began with Liberalism. Liberalism moved on into Modernism, described as follows:

> "Liberalism, thus conceived, calls for the establishment of a political system in which the sovereign people are absolutely free. The sovereign people are completely unrestrained by conscience, by Church, or by God."[177]

There is much more to consider than we have space for here. It is sufficient to report that the liberal doctrines, condemned by Pope Pius IX, are now taught as the basis and doctrine in the Vatican II Church.

---

176   An Outline History of the Church, Page: 533
177   An Outline History of the Church, Page: 535

But My Priest Never Said the Novus Ordo

For this he deserves praise. Several priests never said the Novus Ordo. However, did he ever accept any of the five antipopes of the Vatican II apostate church?[178] If so, he became a schismatic, thus incurring all of the results enumerated above. The presumption of law is that we must presume this has occurred for the good of the Church. We are not judging his soul, but the results of his outward actions. Only a pope can declare to the contrary. No priest can demonstrate that he has departed completely from the Vatican II Church, and obedience to its heretical antipopes. In fact, few priests today claim that Benedict XVI certainly is not pope. Most of the Traditionalist priests hold to some form of validity for Joseph Ratzinger's claim to the papacy, no matter how remote this claim may be.

---

178 This church has usurped the name of Catholic and has not given itself a name. However, many have given it various names from Montinian church to bastard church. All of which seem quite appropriate.

Conclusion

*"To adhere to a false Bishop of Rome
is to be out of Communion with the Church."*[179]

We must conclude that all of the priests and bishops have defected from the Faith by their association with the Vatican II church, in one way or another. Therefore, they have lost all authority in the Church. They must not celebrate Mass or confer the Sacraments for any reason, except danger of death. They must seek the Pope in order to be reconciled with the Church. The bishops departed on, or before, December 4, 1963. Priests likewise departed on, or long before, April 3, 1969 when Montini promulgated <u>Missale Romanum</u>. Many may wish that there was an exception, preferably, their own priest, but this can only be proven in an ecclesiastical court of the Apostolic See. Until this is done, we must presume no exception exists.

Aren't you denying the necessity of the priesthood, and therefore, the episcopate? As stated above, there is an exception. There are those priests and bishops who do not have any knowledge of Vatican II. Therefore, they cannot be held accountable for what has happened there. That God has preserved at least one bishop is without question. To state the contrary is most likely heretical. It is most likely that this bishop (or hopefully more than one) exist in either Russia or China. Due to persecution they are unable to make contact with the Apostolic See.[180] Due to the ongoing persecution, they have been unable to determine where the Pope really is. Subsequently, they have not made contact. Let us pray this soon ends.

---

179   Saint Cyprian
180   Rumors have circulated that when political things eased they made contact with Apostate Rome, and have seen that this is not the Catholic Church.

Are Catholics Catholic?

Above we see that the second largest denomination in the Untied States are lapsed Catholics. That is those who were baptized into the Catholic Church or into the Vatican II sect, which claims the name of Catholic. These people, if asked, call themselves Catholic, but are they really. Is it sufficient to claim a name to actually be something? Let us look at the statistics and then draw the proper conclusions. First of all 68 million people claim to be practicing Catholics, that is they enter a church building on a regular basis. Some of these are Chreasters, that is they show up for Christmas and Easter in a church building. Now the Commandment of the Church requires a Catholic to assist at Mass on all Holydays of Obligation, which includes all Sundays and several other major Feast Days. And so these are not truly practicing Catholics.

Let us review the statistics reported above in the Introduction. 88% believe birth control is acceptable and 66% see nothing wrong with per-marital sex. Therefore at most only 12% of those who claim to be Catholic actually are, for to believe birth-control is permitted is an act of heresy and we have seen that heretics are no longer Catholics. Almost 50% think there is nothing wrong with homosexual practices, while half reject the infallibility of of the Pope. 31% of the abortions are performed on women, who claim to be Catholic, but are not really. And we can see that few who claim the name of Catholic are truly catholic, believing all that Jesus teaches through His holy Church.

Let us look to Washington DC. Six of the nine Supreme Court Justices claim to be Catholic, and yet Roe versus Wade has not been overturned. The current Secretary of Health and Human Services (Kathleen Sebelius) is nominally Catholic, and yet pro-abortion. In fact, the Vice President (Joe Biden) is likewise a pro-abortion nominal Catholic. How many nominal Catholics are pro-abortion?

Is Jesus Really Present?

29% of those who claim to be Catholics believe they are receiving bread and wine in Holy Communion, which represent the spirit and teachings of Jesus Christ. 24% believe that when receiving Holy Communion that they are receiving the Body and Blood of Jesus Christ which has become so because of their personal belief. 10% believe that they are receiving bread and wine, in which Jesus is somehow truly present. This is consubstantiation, and possibly transelementation. 8% hold some other belief, while 30% believe the Catholic doctrine of transubstantiation.

The Catholic doctrine is that when a priest pronounces the proper words of consecration over true bread and wine with the proper intention, the bread and wine change substantially into the Body and Blood of Jesus Christ. Jesus remains as such, until the accidents of bread and wine fall away through digestion or some other cause. Recall, though, that in the Novus Ordo Missae, the form of consecration has been changed substantially and thus Jesus is not truly present, so it is logical that belief in the Real Presence of Jesus in the Blessed Sacrament would also fall away. There are many theories being spread in the Vatican II sect not only among the laity, but by priests and bishops of that sect.

Some teach that Jesus becomes present in some manner, when the priest elevates the bread and wine and the faithful unite and with the bread and wine somehow form the Mystical Body of Jesus Christ of which the bread and wine are mere symbols. Others teach Jesus become present at the moment of Communion, but only for those who are worthy to receive Jesus, as if Jesus prevents sacrilegious Communions, when Saint Paul teaches the exact opposite doctrine.

Of course, the belief of those who claim to be Catholic vary on many other dogmas of the Divine and Catholic Faith and as we saw above, this is heresy. For many today it is material heresy, but material heresy separates a person from the Catholic

Church. They might be able to save their soul, but material heretics are not Catholic. The solution is to learn everything the Catholic Church teaches and accept it on the authority of Almighty God, Who teaches it.

If the faithful of the Vatican II sect do not believe the Catholic Faith do their priests and bishops? Obviously the priests and bishops are not teaching the Catholic Faith sufficiently to end this departure from these truths. Again, there are probably statistics on how many priests believe in the Real Presence. Can a priest who does not believe in transsubstantion validly consecrate, if he uses the correct matter and form in the Indult Mass?

> "Because that, when they knew God, they have not glorified him as God or given thanks: but became vain in their thoughts. And their foolish heart was darkened...Wherefore, God gave them up to the desires of their heart, unto uncleanness: to dishonour their own bodies among themselves. **Who changed the truth of God into a lie** and worshiped and served the creature rather than the Creator, who is blessed for ever. Amen...And, in like manner, the men also, leaving the natural use of the women, have burned in their lusts, one towards another: men with men, working that which is filthy and receiving in themselves the recompense which was due to their error."[181]

---

181   Romans 1:21, 24-5, 27

The Pedophile Crisis

The US statistics show:

$2 billion: Total estimated cumulative financial cost to the Catholic Church[182] in the United States from clergy sex abuse of minors.

$660 million: The amount paid by the Archdiocese of Los Angeles in 2007 to settle 508 sexual abuse lawsuits.

4,392: The total number of all U.S. diocesan and religious priests accused of sexual abuse by 2002.

3,280: The total number of credible allegations reported by dioceses and religious institutes between 2004 and 2007.

5: Number of dioceses declaring bankruptcy because of the scandal.[183]

This is obviously a large problem that has been gravely mishandled by the Novus Ordo Vatican II sect. Much can be said about this problem, such as how Joseph Ratzinger, when asked many years ago about this problem replied that boys will be boys, as if this is in some way natural! Many offer solutions, such as eliminating celibacy for the clergy, as if giving a natural outlet will prevent the unnatural crimes being committed.

We have seen how Vatican II changed the truth into a lie, that is the Catholic Faith into a new non-Catholic Faith with new non-Catholic imitations to replace the Sacraments. As Saint

---

182   This is the Novus Ordo heretical sect under the current Benedict XVI.
183   The Nature and Scope of the Problem of Sexual Abuse of Minors by Catholic Priests and Deacons in the United States, commonly known as the John Jay Report, is a 2004 report by the John Jay College of Criminal Justice.

Paul reported, when we lose the Catholic Faith, loss of morals is not far behind.

Let us look at how the Catholic Church deals with Pedophilia as opposed to the Church that was born at Vatican II.

1917 Code of Canon law of the Catholic Church: "If they (clerics) have committed an offense against the sixth commandment with minors under sixteen years of age, or been guilty of adultery, rape, bestiality, sodomy, traffic in vice, or incest with blood-relatives or relations by marriage in the first degree, they shall be suspended, declared infamous, deprived of every office, benefice, dignity, or position that they may hold, and in more grievous cases they shall be deposed."[184]	1983 Code of Canon Law of Antipope John Paul II "A cleric who has offended in other ways against the sixth commandment of the Decalogue, if the crime was committed by force, or by threats, or in public, or with a minor under the age of sixteen years, is to be punished with just penalties, not excluding dismissal from the clerical state if the case so warrants." [185]

The Catholic Church provides that a cleric should be immediately dismissed from any office they may hold, whereas the 1983 Code provides only that they should be punished with a just penalty. In practice, the Vatican II Church considers a move across town a just penalty.

The Fifth Lateran Council decreed: "If anyone, cleric or layman, be convicted of the crime on account of which the anger of God came upon the children of unbelief," (i.e. pedophilia) "let he be punished in accordance with the sacred canon or the civil law respectively."[186]

---

184 A Practical Commentary On The Code Of Canon Law, Volume 2, Canon 2359, Page: 550
185 The Code of Canon Law, Page: 247
186 Disciplinary Decrees of the General Councils, Page: 496

Saint Pius V went further:

"Therefore, wishing to pursue with greater rigor than we have exerted since the beginning of our pontificate, we establish that any priest or member of the clergy, either secular or regular, who commits such an execrable crime, by force of the present law be deprived of every clerical privilege, of every post, dignity and ecclesiastical benefit, and having been degraded by an ecclesiastical judge, **let him be immediately delivered to the secular authority to be put to death, as mandated by law as the fitting punishment for laymen who have sunk into this abyss.**"[187]

When this was legislated, it was quite probable this meant the death penalty, and this decree is unprecedented, since the Church normally reserves the judgment and punishment of clergy to herself.

---

[187] www.traditioninaction.org/religious/n009rp_HomosexualPriests.htm

Extra Ecclesiam Nulla Salus

Apocatastasis is the doctrine that eventually all intelligent beings, angels and men will be saved. This proposition goes back to the time of the Fathers of the Church and is one reason why Origen was never canonized a Saint, for he held this proposition. More recently the founders of Protestantism are claimed to have held this position, which has become more and more acceptable and politically correct in the world today.

"The Church is the People that God gathers together in the whole world." says the CCC of the Vatican II Church.[188] Vatican II defines their church as the People of God. <u>Lumen Gentium</u>[189] of Vatican II states: "Finally, those who have not yet received the Gospel are related in various ways to the people of God." In essence Vatican II declares that all mankind are in some way part of the People of God. So when a member of this church which falsely claims the name of Catholic says: "as Saviour wills that all men be saved,"[190] they mean that all souls will be saved regardless of what they believe and how immoral they live.

<u>Lumen Gentium</u> continues:

> "In the first place we must recall the people to whom the testament and the promises were given and from whom Christ was born according to the flesh. On account of their fathers this people remains most dear to God, for God does not repent

---

188   CCC stands for <u>Catechism of the Catholic Church</u> of the Vatican II Church and we will use the abbreviation CCC. This is from paragraph 752. Note well this was infallibly approved by Karol Wojtyla as Antipope John Paul II and approved for printing by then Cardinal Ratzinger. Therefore if it contains any error, this must be attributed to these two men.
189   <u>Vatican Council II: The Conciliar and Post Conciliar Documents</u>, Page: 367
190   <u>Vatican Council II: The Conciliar and Post Conciliar Documents</u>, Page: 367

of the gifts He makes nor of the calls He issues. But the plan of salvation also includes those who acknowledge the Creator. In the first place amongst these there are the Mohammedans, who, professing to hold the faith of Abraham, along with us adore the one and merciful God, who on the last day will judge mankind. Nor is God far distant from those who in shadows and images seek the unknown God, for it is He who gives to all men life and breath and all things, and as Saviour wills that all men be saved. Those also can attain to salvation who through no fault of their own do not know the Gospel of Christ or His Church, yet sincerely seek God and moved by grace strive by their deeds to do His will as it is known to them through the dictates of conscience."

We saw previously that this quote from <u>Lumen Gentium</u> means that they believe that Allah, the god of Islam is the one true God. So, when they say People of God it should be interpreted as the People of Allah. And according to Vatican II, all men will be saved, for all men are part of the People of Allah.

What Does the Catholic Church Teach on Salvation?

There are some who claim the name of Catholic who pronounce all who have not been baptized with water are damned for all eternity. At the other end of the spectrum are those who believe in Apocatastasis, or the eventual salvation of all. Both propositions are heretical, because the truth is to be found in the middle. God has not created anyone for eternal damnation; we do this to our own self by refusing to do His will. Every person receives all the grace they need in order to obtain eternal salvation and will be judged upon what they have been given by Almighty God. The Council of Trent teaches:

> "In these words a description of the justification of a sinner is given as being a translation from that state in which man is born a child of the first Adam to the state of grace and of the 'adoption of sons' (Romans 8:15) of God through the second Adam, Jesus Christ, our Saviour; and this translation after the promulgation of the Gospel cannot be effected except through the laver of regeneration,[191] **or a desire for it**, as it is written: 'Unless a man be born again of water and the Holy Ghost, he cannot enter into the kingdom of God.' (John 3:5)"[192]

In our Catechisms this doctrine is presented as Baptism of Blood and Baptism of Desire. This teaching is defended by the Church in official decrees and decisions of the Popes as well as by the Saints throughout history. In the Martyrology we read of men who laid down their lives without Baptism of Water and therefore were baptized in their own blood. To deny the doctrines of Baptism of Blood and Baptism of desire is heretical,

---

[191] The Sources Of Catholic Dogma, # 792, Pages: 247-248
[192] The Sources Of Catholic Dogma, # 796, Pages: 249-250

as the Holy Office determined in the case of Fr. Leonard Feeney.[193]

Fr. Feeney took the position that Baptism of Water is absolutely essential for salvation. This was probably an overreaction to the opposite heresy that was growing in the United States that many of our **separated brethren**[194] are also saved. Pope Pius IX in his Syllabus of Errors condemned the proposition: "We must have at least good hope concerning the eternal salvation of all those who in no wise are in the true Church of Christ."[195] There is hope, but the difficulty of saving oneself out of the Ark of Salvation is great, however it is not impossible as Pope Pius IX also said:

> "And here, beloved Sons and venerable Brothers, we should mention again and censure a very grave error in which some Catholics are unhappily engaged, who believe that men living in error, and separated from the true faith, and from Catholic unity, can attain eternal life. Indeed, this is certainly quite contrary to Catholic teaching. It is known to Us and to you that they who labor in invincible ignorance of our most holy religion and who, zealously keeping the natural law and its precept engraved in the hearts of all by God, and being ready to obey God, live an honest and upright life, since God Who clearly beholds, searches, and knows the minds, souls, thoughts, and habits of all men, because of His great goodness and mercy, will by no means suffer anyone to be punished with eternal torment who

---

193   Canon Law Digest, Volume 3, Pages 525-530
194   Vatican Council II: The Conciliar and Post Conciliar Documents, Pages: 421-423
    A term also found in Lumen Gentium indicated baptized non-Catholics. (See paragraphs 67 and 69.)
195   The Sources Of Catholic Dogma, # 1717, Page: 437

has not the guilt of deliberate sin. But, the Catholic dogma that no one can be saved outside the Catholic Church is well-known; and also that those who are obstinate toward the authority and definitions of the same Church, and who persistently separate themselves from the unity of the Church, and from the Roman Pontiff, the successor of Peter, to whom 'the guardianship of the vine has been entrusted by the Savior,' cannot obtain eternal salvation."[196]

In another Encyclical Pope Pius IX advises not to inquire further into this matter, so let us heed his holy advice.

What we must do is to seek the truth, the whole truth and nothing but the truth. After obtaining the gift of grace to receive the truth, we must act with our intellect, will, conscience, the light of faith, and join visibly with the Church founded by Jesus Christ, **the only Ark of Salvation**. Speculation about what has happened to others is a fruitless waste of time. What we must do is pray for them. If they are in Heaven, the prayers will be redirected to those in need. If they are in Hell, the prayers will be redirected to those in need. And if they are in Purgatory, they greatly need our prayers. Instead, let us proceed to learn the Catholic Faith and then help others to learn this holy Faith, so that we can all find our way from our death bed straight into Heaven. God does wish all of us to take the means to save our souls, so let us do His holy will in this regard!

If we cannot receive the Sacraments actually, let us receive them spiritually as we are advised in the Catechism. Are we not advised to make a Perfect Act of Contrition in the Catechism, if we cannot confess our sins to a **duly authorized priest?**[197] Are we not advised to make Spiritual Communions,

---

196   Quanto conficiamur moerore, Pope Pius IX, 10 August 1863
197   This shall be discussed further on as the Council of Trent infallibly states that a man must possess both the power of the Order of priesthood as well as authority or jurisdiction over the penitent, which is attached either

especially if we cannot go to Holy Communion? And those who cannot be baptized with water must desire this Baptism and do all in their power to prepare for reception of the Sacrament.

Saint Ambrose says: "I lost him whom I was to regenerate" (i.e. Baptize) "but he did not lose the grace he prayed for."[198] If Baptism of water was absolutely necessary, Jesus would have demonstrated by having Bishop John the Evangelist who was present baptize the Good Thief. The Church would immediately baptize catechumens and then instruct them in the Faith, lest some disaster take them from this life and straight into Hell. The fact that the Church does not do this is sufficient proof of Baptism of Desire for Saint Thomas Aquinas often uses the practice of the Church as a proof of some sacred truth. Fr. Coppens explains this simply:

> "The truth is usually expressed in these words: Out of the Church there is no salvation. The meaning is: 1. That Christ has committed to His Church the dispensation of the ordinary means of sanctification, chiefly true doctrine and the holy Sacraments;[199] 2. That He requires every one to be a member of His Church; so that, if anyone, knowing this obligation, refuses to comply with it, he puts himself out of the way of salvation; 3. That the same holds of anyone who suspects the existence of such responsibility and neglects to examine properly into a matter of so great importance."[200]

---

an Office in the Church or delegated by the Pope or Local Ordinary.
198   www.sedevacantist.com/forums/viewtopic.php?f=2&t=10&view=next
199   It must be remembered that the Sacraments may be validly received outside of the Catholic Church, but objectively they are sacrilegious.
200   A Systematic Study of the Catholic Religion, Page: 67

Chapter 6
A Prophetic Overview

"So extreme is the general perversion that there is room to fear...that the Son of Perdition, of whom the Apostle speaks, has already arrived on Earth."[201] Pope Saint Pius X wrote this in his first Encyclical in 1903.

> "Let no man deceive you by any means: for unless there come a revolt first, and the Man of Sin be revealed, the Son of Perdition who opposeth and is lifted up above all that is called God or that is worshiped, so that he sitteth in the temple of God, shewing himself as if he were God."[202]

Sometime in history, there will be the Antichrist, the Man of Sin, Son of Perdition. This is well demonstrated by Henry Cardinal Manning in his lectures, which are reprinted as The Present Crisis of the Holy See.[203] Sacred Scripture relates that even the elect will be deceived.[204] Imagine such confusion that even God's elect can be deceived by His enemies for a time. There are certain things that must happen sometime in history.

"And the angel took the censer and filled it with the fire of the altar and cast it on the Earth: and there were thunders and voices and lightnings and a great earthquake."[205] This is the seventh seal just before the trumpets of Apocalypse 8 and 9. With the recent tsunami[206] that shook the whole Earth,

---

201   II Thessalonians 3:3. Antichrist is known by various names. Here Saint Paul calls him the Man of Sin and the Son of Perdition. Apocalypse 13 and parts of the book of Daniel also refer to Antichrist.
202   II Thessalonians 2:3-4
203   St. Pius X Press. We recommend that anyone who wishes to understand prophecy from a theological standpoint read this book.
204   Matthew 24:24
205   Apocalypse 8:5
206   December 2004

according to some reports, some are speculating that we are about to enter into these two chapters of the Apocalypse. After detailing many disasters in the Apocalypse, we are told:

> "And the rest of the men, who were not slain by these plagues, did not do penance from the works of their hands, that they should not adore devils and idols of gold and silver and brass and stone and wood, which neither can see nor hear nor walk. Neither did they penance from their murders nor from their sorceries nor from their fornication nor from their thefts."[207]

Whether or not we are about to enter into these tribulations, other tribulations are foretold in Scripture. If there were not to be any tribulations at all, we should still heed this advice from Scripture: "No, I say to you: but except you do penance, you shall all likewise perish."[208]

We must not be like those Saint Paul describes:

> "This know also, that in the last days perilous times shall come. For men shall be lovers of their own selves, covetous, boasters, proud, blasphemers, disobedient to parents, unthankful, unholy, without natural affection, truce-breakers, false accusers, incontinent, fierce, despisers of those that are good, traitors, heady, high-minded, lovers of pleasure more than lovers of God; Having a form of godliness, but denying the power thereof; from such turn away. For of this sort are they, which creep into houses, and lead captive silly women laden with sins, led away with divers lusts and pleasures, ever learning, and never able

---

207 Apocalypse 9:20-21
208 Luke 13:5

to come to the knowledge of the truth."[209]

"Now the Spirit manifestly saith that in the last times some shall depart from the faith, giving heed to spirits of error and doctrines of devils, speaking lies in hypocrisy and having their conscience seared. Forbidding to marry, to abstain from meats, which God hath created to be received with thanksgiving by the faithful and by them that have known the truth."[210]

"Whose coming is according to the working of Satan, in all power and signs and lying wonders: And in all seduction of iniquity to them that perish: because they receive not the love of the truth, that they might be saved. Therefore God shall send them the operation of error, to believe lying: That all may be judged who have not believed the truth but have consented to iniquity."[211]

Saint Paul is referring to the Antichrist, but notice that the reason people perish is that they do not love the truth which is the Divine and Catholic Faith. If we do not love the Catholic Faith and the saving truths it teaches us, then God will send us the operation of error to believe lying.

We must not only respect the Catholic Church founded by Jesus Christ, but we must love it. And what does it mean to love something? When we love something, we think about it all the time. Imagine a couple of young lovers who are preparing for marriage. Their only thought is on their future spouse and making them happy. We must love the Church more strongly than this! What do we do when we love? We expend a lot of effort to please our beloved. And so, we should spend a lot of

---

209   II Timothy 3:1-7
210   I Timothy 4:1-3
211   II Timothy 3:9-11

effort on the Church. We wish to know more about our lover. Therefore, we must spend time learning more about the Church. Can we ever be totally satisfied? Here on Earth it is not possible. For our total satisfaction can only be obtained in Heaven, but we can have a foretaste of these joys in meditating upon the sublime truths of the Holy Catholic Faith.

Let us take this as a warning to know, love, and serve God as the basic catechism advises. And first of all, we must know God by studying about Him from the Catechism as discussed in the first chapter. Only by learning about God and His plan of salvation for us can we love Him. When we love God with our whole heart, soul, mind, body, and strength, then we will serve Him as we ought.[212]

Saint John Eudes reminds us:

> "All the holy Fathers agree that after the death of Antichrist the whole world will be converted, and although some of them assert that the world will last but a few days after his death, while others say a few months, some authorities insist that it will continue to exist many years after. Saint Catherine of Sienna, Saint Vincent Ferrer, Saint Francis of Paula, and a number of other saints have predicted this ultimate universal conversion."[213]

Although we may be in the worst time ever, let us never lose hope. One person said that the whole message of Apocalypse is that we Catholics are on the winning team!

---

212 Deuteronomy 6:5, Matthew 22:37, Mark 12:30, and Luke 10:27
213 The Admirable Heart of Mary, Page: 319

The Worst Time Ever

"For there shall be then great tribulation, such as hath not been from the beginning of the world until now, neither shall be. And unless those days had been shortened, no flesh should be saved: but for the sake of the elect those days shall be shortened."[214]

"But at that time shall Michael rise up, the great prince, who standeth for the children of thy people: and a time shall come such as never was from the time that nations began even until that time. And at that time shall thy people be saved, every one that shall be found written in the book."[215]

"For in those days shall be such tribulations as were not from the beginning of the creation which God created until now: neither shall be. And unless the Lord had shortened the days, no flesh should be saved: but, for the sake of the elect which he hath chosen, he hath shortened the days."[216]

Notice that both Gospels state that this will be the worst time in history, but both Gospels say: neither shall be, indicating that better times will come after these great trials. I recommend reading all three Gospel accounts in Matthew 24, Mark 13, and Luke 19.

---

214 Matthew 24:21-22
215 Daniel 12:1
216 Mark 13:19-20

Antichrist

Much has been written on Antichrist,[217] especially in the last half a century. There is not space here to consider Antichrist in detail. At least three sources indicate that Antichrist has already come and gone.[218] If Saint Pius X's fears are justified, then we must presume that Antichrist has come and gone. Many will immediately object. "We did not see and recognize him?" if you are suppose to have recognized him how was he suppose to be like a thief in the night?[219] The reason is simple: Many are following the Protestant theory that Antichrist will be a one-world dictator who would be the worst in history. However, to qualify as Antichrist, **Antichrist must be a spiritual leader.** Antichrist's job description entails attracting souls from what is sweet, delicious, and satisfying to the intellect (ie the truth) to what is bitter, sour, and emptiness (heresy). We must remember that Jesus Christ came as a spiritual King, establishing a spiritual kingdom, the Catholic Church. His Kingdom consists of three parts:

1. The Church Triumphant in Heaven
2. The Church Suffering in Purgatory
3. The Church Militant here on Earth.[220]

---

217 "A designation of Christ's chief antagonist, who will precede His second coming and the end of the world, and whose activity will be directly connected with a widespread apostasy from the Christian faith. He will be an individual human personality, marked by utter lawlessness, self-deification, hatred of Christian truth, and rivalry with Christ through mock-miracles. He will cause the fall of many, but be destroyed by Christ." (A Catholic Dictionary, Page: 24)

218 Pope Saint Pius X as indicated above, The Man of Sin, History of the Church also covers this.

219 "The thief cometh not, but for to steal, and to kill, and to destroy." (John 10:10)

220 Let us remember that all of us enrolled in an army when we were baptized to fight against principalities and powers, and at Confirmation we were declared ready to go on the front lines.

Antichrist is considered in several sections of Sacred Scripture.[221] Here let us consider just one of the things Antichrist does. And it was magnified even to their prince of the strength: and it took away from him the continual sacrifice, and cast down the place of his sanctuary. And strength was given him against the continual sacrifice, because of sins: and truth shall be cast down on the ground, and he shall do and shall prosper."[222]

---

221 I John 2:18,22
    I John 4:3
    II John 1:7
    Apocalypse 13:1-8
    II Timothy 3
    Daniel 7, 11 and 12 to name a few.
222 Daniel 8:11-12

The Holy Sacrifice of the Mass Will Cease Entirely For Some Time

"In it was shown her" (Anna Catherine Emmerich) "the Holy Mass as the line of demarcation between men in time and in eternity; and she saw also its cessation at the time of Antichrist."[223] Saint Alphonsus[224] confirms that the Mass will cease entirely for a time, referring to Daniel:

"And it was magnified even to their prince of the strength: and it took away from him the continual sacrifice, and cast down the place of his sanctuary. And strength was given him against the continual sacrifice, because of sins: and truth shall be cast down on the ground, and he shall do and shall prosper."[225]

Saint Francis de Sales mentions this as well.[226] Cardinal Manning proves that this is infallibly true:

"The Holy Fathers who have written upon the subject of Antichrist, and of the prophecies of Daniel, without a single exception, as far as I know, —and they are the Fathers both of the East and of the West, the Greek and the Latin Church—all of them unanimously,—say that in the latter end of the world, during the reign of Antichrist, the holy sacrifice of the altar will cease."[227]

---

223   The Life of Anna Catherine Emmerich, Volume 2, Page: 194
224   The Holy Eucharist, Page: 22
      The Dignity and responsibilities of the Priest, Pages: 211-212
      The Holy Mass, Page: 32
225   Although Saint Alphonsus refers elsewhere in Daniel, this is most appropriate to consider. (Daniel 8:11-12)
226   The Catholic Controversy, Page: 62
227   The Present Crisis of the Holy See, Pages: 49-50
      Remember we determined that when the Fathers of the Church

Therefore, we must conclude that at sometime in history the Mass will cease to be celebrated.

Antichrist takes away the Sacrifice of the Mass because of the sins of those who claim the name of Catholic, but do lie.[228] "And strength was given him against the continual sacrifice, because of sins: and truth shall be cast down on the ground, and he shall do and shall prosper."[229] Is the cause of the cessation of the Sacrifice of the Mass, our failure to learn the truths of the Faith? For Sacred Scripture says: "and truth shall be cast down..."

"And arms shall stand on his part, and they shall defile the sanctuary of strength, and shall take away the continual sacrifice, and they shall place there the abomination unto desolation."[230] Notice that the continual sacrifice is taken away so that the abomination of desolation can be put in its place. Based upon all of this, many identify Giovanni Baptiste Montini as Antipope Paul VI, The Antichrist, since he replaced the Sacrifice of the Mass with the Novus Ordo Missae.

---

unanimously agree on how to interpret Sacred Scripture, their interpretation is infallibly true.
228   Apocalypse 3:9
229   Daniel 8:12
230   Daniel 11:31

Objections

Montini never performed any miracles. The latter part of Apocalypse 13 says the Antichrist will perform miracles. Here is where we need to read carefully. Apocalypse 13, verses 1-8 talk about a beast. Then notice a transition.

> "And I saw another beast coming up out of the Earth: and he had two horns, like a lamb: and he spoke as a dragon. And he executed all the power of the former beast in his sight. And he caused the Earth and them that dwell therein to adore the first beast, whose wound to death was healed."[231]

Notice it is this beast, not Antichrist, who performs miracles.

Isn't Antichrist supposed to kill the two witnesses of Apocalypse 11? Apocalypse 11 deals with the two witnesses who preach for three and a half years. Many hold these two witnesses to be Enoch and Elias.[232]

> "And when they shall have finished their testimony, the beast that ascendeth out of the abyss shall make war against them and shall overcome them and kill them. And their bodies shall lie in the streets of the great city which is called spiritually, Sodom and Egypt: where their Lord also was crucified."[233]

Nowhere else is reference made to the beast from the abyss. There are beasts in Daniel and The Apocalypse, one of

---

231 Apocalypse 13:11-12
232 A minority opinion say Elias and Moses. I personally think Enoch and Elias because neither has yet died.
233 Apocalypse 11:7-10

whom is Antichrist proper. Could this beast from the abyss be the second beast of Apocalypse 13:11-18? If so, then the two witnesses will soon appear, as will this second beast. This second beast will possibly canonize Antipope Paul VI as a saint of the Novus Ordo Church, thus canonizing Vatican II and the New Rites of the Sacraments. And all we have been discussing above.

Aren't You Speculating?

> "Even if Catholics faithful to Tradition are reduced to a handful, they are the ones who are the Church of Jesus Christ."[234]

We must of course always conform our opinion of Sacred Scripture to the opinion of the Church. However, there are several opinions on the meaning of some parts of Scripture. Also, with prophecy, it becomes crystal clear after the fact, while it remains obscure until that time. That the Mass has been taken away and the abomination of desolation set in its place, should be obvious.[235] There is not space in this booklet to consider prophesy in detail. Prophesy must be left for another book, or to others.

We need to consider one last point. "Let no man deceive you by any means: for unless there come a revolt first, and the man of sin be revealed, the Son of Perdition..."[236] This revolt is also called by some, the falling away, or the great apostasy from the Greek word used here. The Latin word from the Vulgate translates departure. This departure is considered by many authorities to be so large that only a few remain in the Church, possibly even a mere handful. Since this is the worst time ever,[237] couldn't this handful be a small number indeed? "And they that remain of the trees of His forest shall be so few, that they shall easily be numbered, and a child shall write them down."[238]

---

234 <u>Saint Athanasius Letter: Nicene and Post-Nicene Fathers</u>, Volume 4, Pages: 550-551
235 This is discussed in greater detail in other places and we will not go into that much detail here.
236 II Thessalonians 2:3
237 Matthew 24:21-22; Daniel 12:1; Mark 13:19-20
238 Isaias 10:19

Conclusion

The main point to remember is that there will be a terrible time in history that will cause many to lose the faith. The **Great Apostasy** causes all but a handful of people to depart from the Church.[239] Even the elect will be deceived.[240] Antichrist will appear and take away the Sacrifice of the Mass. This will happen because of the sins of those who are Catholics in name only, but do not live the Faith. Fortunately, after all of these trials there will be a universal conversion to the Catholic Faith.

---

239   II Thessalonians 3
240   Matthew 24:24

And Another Beast Rose

In Apocalypse, the latter part of the 13th chapter is devoted to a second beast, who is not Antichrist, but apparently a successor. Just who will be this beast? With the death of John Paul II the Great Deceiver, it is certain that he was not this beast. It appears likely that Joseph Ratzinger also is not this beast, although he continues the policies of his four perfidious predecessors. True, recently, he has taken a conservative turn, putting away the Jansenist Cross instituted by Antipope Paul VI, and carried by Antipopes John Paul I and II. He has also put away his radical pallium in favor of a more conservative one. This alone is an innovation, as an Archbishop receives a pallium with his office, which he keeps until death. Of course, why shouldn't these men depart from tradition in small things, since they have departed from the Divine and Catholic Faith?

Even the carrying of the cross in place of a crosier is a departure from two millennia of tradition. Peter left his staff on a visit outside of Rome and never carried one afterwards. In light of this, the Pope does not carry a staff or crosier, but processes with nothing in his hands. Tradition holds that the crosier is a sign of authority, but of limited authority, which is why a bishop carries it in his own diocese, but nowhere else. The Pope, whose jurisdiction is unlimited, does not carry the crozier. In fact, there is much to the symbolism of this new church founded by Roncalli and Montini, which continues today under Fr. Ratzinger.

Yes, Ratzinger was consecrated bishop in the New Rite of Ordination, which is substantially different from the Catholic Rite of Ordination. Therefore Ratzinger is not a Catholic Bishop or even a non-Catholic Bishop. Ironically, by the laws of his own church, he is not pope of his own church. Antipope Paul VI established the Papal Election Law of the Vatican II Church.[241] In this law, a man does not become Pope, until he is consecrated

---

241   Romano Pontifici Eligendo, Paragraph 88-89

Bishop. The 1983 Code of Canon Law confirms this. Finally Antipope John Paul II the Great Deceiver promulgated his own election law.[242] While it is indeed a doctrine of faith that the power of the Supreme Pontiff derives directly from Christ, whose earthly Vicar he is, it is also certain that this supreme power in the Church is granted to him "by means of lawful election accepted by him, together with episcopal consecration."[243] This is a substantial change to almost two millennia of tradition as stated in the 1917 Code of Canon Law. "The Roman Pontiff legitimately elected obtains, from the moment he accepts election, the full power of supreme jurisdiction by divine right."[244] Since Joseph Ratzinger is not a valid Bishop, by the laws of his own Church, he can in no way be Pope! It should be noted that the tradition of the Church, which is of divine law that the Pope receives authority the moment he accepts election cannot be changed by the Church, because Divine Law cannot be changed.

The Prophet Isaias of these times says: "And they that remain of the trees of his forest shall be so few, that they shall easily be numbered, and a child shall write them down." Henry Cardinal Manning also reported that the Great Apostasy must necessarily come at some time in history. And this Great Apostasy, according to Saint Nicholas of Flue, will devastate the Church so much that:

> "The Church will sink still deeper until she will at last seem to be extinguished, and the succession of Peter and the other Apostles to have expired. After that she will be victoriously exalted in the sight of all doubters. The Church will be punished because the majority of her members-high and

---

242 Universi Dominici Gregis, Paragraphs 88-89
243 A Practical Commentary On The Code Of Canon Law, Volume 1, Canon 332, Page: 135
244 A Practical Commentary On The Code Of Canon Law, Volume 1, Canon 219, Page: 98

low-will become so perverted."²⁴⁵

Nearly all the Bishops will desert the Church which Christ founded. Thus making it appear that the Apostolic Succession ceases to exist.²⁴⁶ Prophecy of Blessed Tomasuccio:

> "By about twelve years shall the millennium have passed when the resplendent mantle of legitimate power shall emerge from the shadows where it was being kept by the schism. And beyond harm from the one who is blocking the door of salvation, for his deceitful schism shall have come to an end. And the mass of the faithful shall attach itself to the worthy Shepherd, who shall extricate each one from error and restore to the Church its beauty. He shall renew it."

If this prophecy is true, then these evil times, which began in 1958 shall end with a full restoration of the Church in 2012. Of course, as Catholics, we should restore ourselves fully to the Catholic Church now and prepare for this glorious restoration, which we know will come at some time as seen above!

---

245   The Prophets And Our Times, Page: 163
246   It is a matter of Faith that the Apostles will have a continual line of successors to their mission and authority until the end of time as the Vatican Council declares in 1870. (The Sources Of Catholic Dogma, # 1825, Page: 453) So these words must be read carefully. Those who hold the Office of Bishop have an inherent right to receive the Order of Bishop.

Chapter 7
Reaction to the Changes

> Latin's gone, peace is too,
> Singin' and shoutin' from every pew,
> Altar's turned 'round, priest is too;
> Commentator's yellin', "page twenty-two."
> Communion rails goin', stand up straight!
> Kneelin'; suddenly went outta date.
> Processions are formin' in every aisle,
> Salvation's organized single file.
> Rosary's out, psalms are in.
> Hardly ever hear a word against sin.
> Listen to the lector, hear how he reads.
> Please stop rattlin' them rosary beads.
> Padre's lookin' puzzled, doesn't know his part;
> Used to know the whole deal in Latin by heart.
> I hope all the changes are just about done,
> That they don't drop Bingo before I've won.[247]

This is an apt description of the happenings in Catholic churches in the 1960's. "Further, the general reform of the liturgy will be better received by the faithful if it is accomplished gradually..."[248] If the Novus Ordo Missae had been introduced suddenly, half the people would have headed for the exits. So the changes were introduced over time. Actually, **the changes** began prior to the approval of the Liturgy decree by the Second Ecumenical Council of the Vatican. On his own authority, John XXIII had added Saint Joseph's name to the Canon, contrary to the clear prescriptions of Pope Saint Pius V's bull <u>Quo Primum</u>. This Bull forbade any change in the Mass.

---

247 <u>The Updated Church: a Conservative's Comment</u>, T. Lincoln Bouscaren, April 1965, <u>Homiletic and Pastoral Review</u>
248 <u>Vatican Council II: The Conciliar and Post Conciliar Documents</u>, Page: 46

Also, the Prayers at the foot of the altar had been shortened. Soon the vernacular began to creep into the readings at Mass.

There is a story about cooking a frog. Drop a frog into boiling water and he will jump out. Place the frog in cool water, and then raise the heat slowly, he will stay in and cook. The Enemy knew that there would be a reaction to the institution of the Novus Ordo. This is the reason why the liturgy was slowly brought into the vernacular, and modified, until one day the Novus Ordo was instituted in its place. This was the final change. Another name for this process is gradualism, first used by the Socialists and Communists.

The devil hates the Mass. Many began to believe that the Devil was gaining the upper hand when Kumbayah replaced the Kyrie, when a table replaced the altar, and when the Mass was replaced with a meal. The Devil knew that there would be a reaction to the implementation of the Novus Ordo Missae. Some simply would not accept this in place of the Latin Mass.

In 1970, Brothers Francis Schuckardt and Dennis Chicoine began going around the country speaking to groups about the Novus Ordo Missae. They spoke against the Novus Ordo. They concluded by saying to their audiences that anyone who went to a Novus Ordo service after hearing their speech would commit mortal sin. Soon they found a priest to join with them. They also found an Old-Catholic bishop. They had the priest reconcile the Old-Catholic bishop with the Church.[249] This old-Catholic bishop ordained Schuckardt to the priesthood, and consecrated him bishop. Br. Dennis was also ordained. Thus, the Congregation of Mary Immaculate was born, also known as the CMRI.[250] This organization worked in Coeur d'Alene, Idaho. CMRI was one step ahead of the Society of Saint Pius X in

---

249 Remember that this is reserved to the Local Ordinary, and further only the Pope can restore an old-Catholic bishop to exercise of the priesthood. This is only done after a complete seminary course to make sure they know what the Catholic Faith teaches.

250 The foundation of an organization like this is reserved to the Local Ordinary of the place where it is founded. Also, each Ordinary must give permission for such an organization to move into his diocese.

obtaining a vacant seminary in Spokane, Washington in the late '70's.

However, the CMRI was not what many people wanted. People wanted priests that had been ordained in the Catholic Church. Many departed from the Novus Ordo to minister to these people in the early '70's. One of the first not to celebrate the Novus Ordo was Fr. James Dunphy. He went coast to coast and border to border in the United States. He simply told people to reject newer things, and that there were no real answers to the problems. He did encourage spirituality, but soon he was grounded by his superiors. Fr. James Dunphy stayed home in Saint Louis. This is where he remains to this day. Other priests left the Novus Ordo and provided various forms of the Latin Mass to Catholics throughout the world. However, these were seen as a dead end street, as some day, they must all die. No, there had to be a long term solution.

On Christmas Eve, 1971, a conversation started in Econe, Switzerland between Archbishop Marcel Lefebvre and Fr. Guerard des Lauriers about whether it was better to use the Latin Mass, or the Novus Ordo. Fr. Guerard des Lauriers, who is said to have written the <u>Ottaviani Intervention</u>, asked: "Monseigneur, it is a pity that, while maintaining Tradition, you have been celebrating something called a **New Mass?**"[251] Thus, the Apostles of Jesus and Mary became the center of the Traditionalist Movement.[252] Lefebvre was to cement his position when he declared the Novus Ordo a bastard rite.[253] Here was a bishop, ordained and consecrated in the Catholic Church

---

251   This information comes from an article by Fr. Des Lauriers, "Monseigneur, We Do Not Want This Peace." The Society now admits that the Novus Ordo was celebrated there, but give a different date for its removal.

252   Most will know this organization by its public title. The Society of Saint Pius X.

253   <u>Apologia Pro Marcel Lefebvre</u>, Volume 1, Page: 262, quoting from the sermon at Lille August 29, 1976. Many of the quotes are translations from the French, and some of the translations are not that good. Please bear with us as we have chosen to use the exact translation circulated.

standing up against the Novus Ordo. Lefebvre proceeded to found seminaries and priories throughout the world to serve the requests of Traditionalists.[254] Lefebvre promised to provide solid well trained priests to serve the needs of Traditionalists.

Lefebvre decided to hold to the position that Paul VI and then John Paul II were valid Popes, although they permitted many things to happen which were unacceptable. Lefebvre claimed that Vatican II was merely a pastoral council. Therefore, it must be interpreted in the light of tradition.

"The heresy which is now being born will become the most dangerous of all; the exaggeration of the respect due to the Pope and the illegitimate extension of his infallibility."[255] Fr. Le Floch was head of the French Seminary in Rome when Lefebvre was a seminarian there. Lefebvre applied this principle to Vatican II and its spirit. Lefebvre declared that none of these things were infallible. In fact, he went so far as to declare that Vatican II was only a pastoral council, and therefore never defined anything infallibly. And so, Catholics could happily maintain Paul VI as their Pope while disobeying his wish and hope that we accept the Novus Ordo Missae and the accompanying new Sacramental Rites, and the New Religion they represent. The lines were drawn when Paul VI suspended Lefebvre. Lefebvre declared that he must continue to defend tradition, hence the term Traditionalist. The term Traditionalist has been applied to all who reject the Novus Ordo, and accept the Latin Mass in some form.

The Society of Saint Pius X founded by Lefebvre was not the only place to find the Traditionalist Mass.[256] In the early to

---

254   Basically, a Traditionalist is commonly held to be anyone who wants a Latin Mass, as opposed to those happy with the Novus Ordo. There are various forms of the Latin Mass in use today. However, since John Paul II's death, he has been called a Traditionalist because he held to traditional doctrine on a few moral issues. This has introduced confusion into this term because Traditionalists reject most of John Paul II's doctrines. Especially those doctrines on religious liberty.
255   Fr. Le Floch, head of the French Seminary in 1926.
256   The Latin Mass will be referred to as the Traditionalist Mass. There

mid 1970's, many priests departed from the Novus Ordo in order to serve the many Traditionalists throughout the world. A few priests joined with Lefebvre in his Society, but many more remained independent. These priests simply set up a chapel, or chapels, and served them. A de facto [257] emergency was implicitly declared and these priests ministered as if they had full approval by the Church to do so. For the young men wanting to be priests, there was only one route: Lefebvre. Lefebvre refused to ordain for other than his own Society and a few sympathetic upshot monasteries in Europe.

With Lefebvre's continual insistence that Paul VI was Pope, and then, John Paul I and II, people began to wonder. How could a true Pope give us a bastard rite of the mass? Thus, increasingly, priests and people began to reject Paul VI's claim to the papacy. This included a number of Lefebvre's own followers.[258] But what are these priests and people to do for priests in the future?

---

are various forms in use by the various Traditionalists.
257   By the facts at hand an emergency was declared *de facto*.
258   In fact, reports to this day indicate a number of Society of Saint Pius X followers, and even some of their priests reject the claim of John Paul II to the Papacy. One of their bishops has declared that the next papal election held in Rome, when John Paul II dies or resigns, will be invalid. Since this did not come to pass, we can presume he is now waiting for Benedict XVI to die or is a dishonest man.

Theories on the Papacy

Before continuing, we must discuss the three main theories ventured about whether or not John XXIII and Paul VI, and their successors, John Paul I and II and Benedict XVI, were in fact, Popes. The first theory is that of Lefebvre: They were merely bad popes. We are fully justified in resisting them. We should, however, obey their lawful decrees, but who is to decide? Lefebvre decided to accept the reduction of the Communion fast to one hour. This was instituted by Paul VI. Lefebvre also accepted all of the changes introduced by John XXIII, except the omission of Psalm 42 in the Prayers at the Foot of the Altar.[259] Many who hold this position have accepted the concessions granted by John Paul II. Thus, they returned to the Vatican II Church, while being allowed to have the John XXIII Missal. Let us remember: "To adhere to a false Bishop of Rome is to be out of communion with the Church."[260]

The second theory is that by the implemention of the Novus Ordo Missae, Paul VI became a heretic. Thus, Paul VI instantly lost the papacy. The followers of this theory are called sedevacantists, taken from the Latin words describing the situation in the Church when the Pope has died, until a new Pope is elected, a sede vacante. Many are full sedevacantists, although, some are mitigated sedevacantists. These people say they are not totally sure, but they think that there is no pope.

The third theory was proposed by Fr. Guerard des Lauriers, a former professor from Lefebvre's Econe seminary. Des Lauriers proposed that John Paul II is only materially pope, but not formally pope. John Paul II is materially pope because he was elected and physically sits in the Chair of Saint Peter, but not formally pope because he is a heretic.

---

259   A recent discussion with a follower of the Society of Saint Pius X indicates that they are no longer obliged to observe the fast laws of the Church. The Society of Saint Pius X accepts the elimination of fasting implemented by Paul VI.
260   Saint Cyprian

Archbishop Peter Martin Ngo-Dihn Thuc

There is a lot said about this man. There is not space here to consider all of the rumors about this man, but we must reflect on the facts. First, Archbishop Ngo-Dihn[261] was a friend of Archbishop Lefebvre. Reports are that Lefebvre invited him to teach at Econe.

In late 1976, a seer from Palmar de Troya, Spain, Clemente Dominguez, approached Lefebvre. Clemente Dominguez stated that the Blessed Virgin Mary had told him to be ordained and consecrated. Instead of dismissing him, Lefebvre told Clemente to go to Archbishop Ngo-Dihn who went to Palmar and performed the requested ordinations and consecrations.[262] Ngo-Dihn repented when Paul VI excommunicated him, and he was received back into the Novus Ordo Church. He was to remain with the Novus Ordo Church until 1982. Then he declared that the Papacy was vacant. Now the independent priests had an alternative.

It was becoming increasingly obvious that Novus Ordo Rome would not give in to the Traditionalists any time soon. The future of Traditionalism required more than a steady supply of new priests. Traditionalism required bishops hopefully to carry on the apostolic succession. It was arranged in the spring of 1981 for Archbishop Ngo-Dihn to consecrate Fr. Des Lauriers as bishop. However, Fr. Des Lauriers began promoting his papal theory. Thus, two Mexican priests were brought to Europe to be consecrated bishops in the fall of 1981. To justify these later consecrations, Ngo-Dihn declared the papacy vacant in early 1982. Archbishop Ngo-Dihn gave rise to two groups of Traditionalists. The first group accepts the theory of Fr. Des Lauriers: John Paul II is materially pope, thus impeding any permanent solution. The second group is known as

---

261 In Vietnamese, the family name comes before one's given name. Catholics add a Baptismal name at the front.
262 There is a great deal of circumstantial evidence to link Lefebvre with Palmar de Troya at this time.

sedevacantists. They have rightfully followed Archbishop Ngo-Dihn Thuc in declaring that John Paul II is a usurper of the papacy. However, these two groups do not have unity, even among their own ranks. They are divided and subdivided.

It should be noted that no Bishop can be legitimately consecrated without a mandate from the Pope, and that all Bishops involved are excommunicated by the Law of the Church without any need of further declaration.

The Society of Saint Pius X Splits

In the late 1970's, many of Lefebvre's American priests had become de facto sede vacantists, but they remained within the Society. Lefebvre chastised them. But because he needed priests, he retained them. Finally, by the spring of 1983, some of Lefebvre's machinations had become too much for these priests. But they had a problem: They had five men in the seminary they wanted ordained. Unfortunately, these priests had commissioned an article: <u>Two Bishops In Every Garage</u>, denouncing the Thuc-line[263] bishops. This route now was not open to them. And so, they departed from the Society immediately after the first two of these men were ordained priests. To deepen the scandal Lefebvre required all of his priests to vow acceptance of Wojtyla as their pope, John Paul II. All of these men signed this vow, but they immediately rejected it.

Were their complaints unfounded? No, some were well founded. For instance, Lefebvre admitted priests ordained in the New Rite of Ordination into the Society. He did not require conditional reordination in the true Rite of Ordination. They complained that Lefebvre allowed the Modernist decree of John XXIII, <u>Rubricarum Instructum</u> to be implemented in the Society. This reduced many feasts to mere commemorations, while eliminating others. Thus, the changes. began.

The next year the scandal would repeat with three more men vowing acceptance of John Paul II, accepting ordination at Lefebvre's hands, then immediately departing to join with the rest of the priests that had formed the Society of Saint Pius V. This brought their number to twelve.

---

263   Those bishops descending in any way from Archbishop Ngo-Dihn Thuc are called Thuc Bishops. Indeed, there are many such claimants.

The Society Splits Again

Lefebvre announced a successor in 1978. This was an old-Catholic bishop, Georg Schmitz. But, it was becoming obvious that Lefebvre needed to follow Ngo-Dihn's example. Lefebvre needed to consecrate bishops of his own to continue the Society. On June 30, 1988, Lefebvre, assisted by Bishop Antonio de Castro Meyer, consecrated four of his own priests as bishops. Lefebvre formalized his separation from Rome. Or did he? Lefebvre called John Paul II an Antichrist to his dying day. He also called John Paul II his pope, but refused to obey him. There was an immediate reaction. John Paul II excommunicated Lefebvre, de Castro Meyer, and the four new bishops. John Paul II immediately authorized the use of the John XXIII Missal. and accepted many of Lefebvre's followers back into the Novus Ordo Cchurch, thus, forming The Society of Saint Peter. The Society of Saint Peter retains the Latin Mass, but the new priests of this society are ordained by Novus Ordo bishops.

The Indult Mass

A word should be said on the so-called Indult Mass. First of all, it is erroneously reported that this is the Tridentine Mass, when in fact this is the Mass of John XXIII with all of the changes enacted by Antipope Angelo Roncalli. By the insertion of Saint Joseph in the Canon, Roncalli changed this from the Tridentine Mass into a new rite, as stated above. Is the Indult Mass valid? The form remains identical to the Tridentine and to that held by the Church at the Council of Florence. However, we must question the intention in light of the Notitiae mentioned above. Does a priest, who celebrates the Novus Ordo on Saturday Night and an Indult on Sunday morning have the right intention? This can not be said with certainty, especially in light of the fact that to use the Indults of Wojtyla and Ratzinger, one must accept the Novus Ordo Missae as defined by Montini and the Notitiae as certainly valid. It is possible to use the proper words with a perverse intention. Unless the minister declares the contrary, we must presume he intends pro omnibus, for all, when he says pro multis in the indult.

What about the Society of Saint Pius X? Since they now accept the validity of the New Rite of Ordination and have been in regular discussions with the Novus Ordo Church and may also use the John XXIII Mass, we must presume their intention is the same, until the contrary is directly stated! And the moment a priest states he intends differently than prescribed by Antipopes John Paul II the Great Deceiver and/or Benedict XVI, he also declares that he is no longer in union with them and thus has left their church. Having admitted this, he is also admitting that he was once a member of an heretical sect and therefore suspended from all exercise of Holy Orders, until the true Pope personally restores him to full communion with the Catholic Church.

Meanwhile...

While the Lefebvrites were busy with establishing their church, the sede vacantists and the material-formal[264] crowd were busy with their churches. The CMRI founded by Schuckardt split from him. They invited Bishop George Musey to come and conditionally reordain them.[265] Thus, the CMRI was received into mainstream Traditionalism. Soon, Bishop Carmona, one of the two Mexicans consecrated in 1981 by Archbishop Ngo-Dihn Thuc, consecrated one of the CMRI priests as bishop, establishing them as a firm sede vacantist organization.

It would not end here. The Society of Saint Pius V split into three factions. Two factions obtained consecration of one of their own as bishop by a Thucite. The third faction employed another Bishop, Bishop Mendez. Bishop Mendez was a former Bishop of Arecibo, Puerto Rico.

Many groups and theories abound. There is not space to consider them all. However, with the exception of a few remaining independent priests, including some recent converts from the Novus Ordo, the only sources of the so called true Catholic Sacraments stem from either Lefebvre or Ngo-Dihn Thuc.

---

264   This is the theory spoken of above. John Paul II is only materially pope, but not formally pope. This is a return to the original, the preceding section being all new in light of the Notitiae mentioned earlier.
265   Musey stated in the banquet afterwards: This conditional reordination was a mere formality. This places his intention in doubt.

Jurisdiction

From its birth of the Traditionalist, until the early 1980's, Traditionalists simply presumed that their priests had authority to give them the Sacraments. The necessity of Jurisdiction, which is required for the validity of Sacramental absolution in the Confessional, was totally ignored. However, a loophole was found: Canon 209. Fr. Paul Trinchard states:

> "Some argue that, according to the 1917 Code of Canon Law, the Church supplies this essential and absolutely required priestly jurisdiction to individuals or to groups operating outside of the Church. They contend that this code assures them that **ecclesia supplet-extra ecclesiam**. This ultra-liberal thesis is completely false."[266]

He goes on to declare that all Traditionalist priests are merely simplex-priests. That is: priests who can celebrate Mass, as the Cure of Ars was in his early days as a priest. This is similar to the statement by Bishop Daniel Dolan that he is a sacramental bishop.[267] The priesthood has been reduced in Traditionalism to a mere pervayer of the Sacraments without any authority in the Church whatsoever. What is considered important is that the man is validly ordained a priest, and nothing else matters. Men are Sacramental Priests only, and this is sufficient in this time of emergency.

Basically, there are two keys: The superior key of jurisdiction and the key of Orders. Orders can be validly exercised without jurisdiction, as in the case of an Eastern Orthodox Bishop ordaining a priest. But their use is sinful and not legitimate because it is not exercised within the authority of

---

266 <u>Guidelines For Going Outside the Church for Mass and Confession</u>, Page: 19

267 <u>The Smoke of Satan</u>, Pages: 101-102. The Society of Saint Pius X has made a similar assertion in a media brochure.

the Church. Only a pope can permit exceptions or declare on the lawfulness of their use in extraordinary cases.

What many do not realize is that for the valid absolution of sins in the Sacrament of Confession, the priest requires not only the power of Holy Orders, but also the power of jurisdiction over the penitent. This power is possessed by Divine Law by the Pope over the whole Church and the Bishops over their diocese. Church Law extends this power to Pastors over their parishes. All other priests receive their jurisdiction by delegation by the Pope or the Bishop of the Diocese in which they are to hear Confessions. Church Law also delegates certain priests the necessary jurisdiction as part of their office.

Those who are in good faith among the Orthodox are validly absolved in Confession by a special grant of jurisdiction from several Popes. If a priest validly absolves, his authority comes from Jesus Christ through the Pope in an ordinary or extraordinary manner. By the same principle it can be considered that the Popes will also grant such jurisdiction to those who in good faith present them to priests who do not possess such jurisdiction. Thus the Confessions heard by Traditionalists, Old Catholic and others as well as the Orthodox can be presumed to be valid, if the priest also possesses Holy Orders by a special grant from the Roman Pontiffs for the salvation of souls.

Priest Co-Consecrators

Lefebvre and Ngo-Dihn Thuc omitted a part of the Rite of Consecration: the use of co-consecrators. This may seem like a small matter, but this is similar to the practice of the old-Catholics and other heretics who only admit bishops as co-consecrators in consecrating bishops. The Church has consistently insisted on the use of priest co-consecrators when the required three bishops cannot be obtained. The most public example is that of Lefebvre's consecrations on June 30, 1988. Lefebvre was assisted by de Castro Meyer that day, but Lefebvre also had many priests available who could have been a priest co-consecrator. Lefebvre could have employed his first successor, the old-Catholic bishop, Georg Schmitz, if he was available. In the first of Ngo-Dihn Thuc's consecrations there was not another priest present. So one could argue absolute impossibility. But in the second consecration, this was not the case. There were two Mexican priests present. There should have been two consecrations. The first consecration was with Ngo-Dihn Thuc as one priest co-consecrator.[268] The second consecration was with two bishops. In 1808, Pope Pius VII appointed three bishops for the United States. Bishop John Carroll, the first American Bishop, consecrated all three bishops in three ceremonies. The first consecration was with two of the bishops elect, (that is mere priests), as co-consecrators. In the second and third ceremonies, a previous bishop assisted with one of the newly consecrated bishops. This previous bishop was consecrated in 1800 with two priest co-consecrators by Bishop John Carroll.

---

268   Where was des Lauriers? He should have been summoned!

Home Alone

Although this movement started over two decades ago, it only recently was given a name. Traditionalists seeing the confusion, the disunity, and the outright scandal,[269] realized these priests and bishops could not function on behalf of the Catholic Church. They decided to leave these men and simply stay home with their Goffine,[270] Rosary, and Scapular. They await the final trumpet!

Actually this is not as much a movement as a number of people doing similar things in various places throughout the world. They do communicate some and several of these people even maintain websites to promote the heresies of home-alone. One such website proposes the name of 'catacomb Catholic', forgetting that the Catholics in the Catacombs in Rome were centered around the Pope, and when the Pope was martyred, proceeded immediately to elect a successor.

---

269   A whole book could be written on this. A chapter of a book has been written on this. The Smoke Of Satan by Michael W. Cuneo.

270   This is a reference to Fr. Leonard Goffine's Ecclesiastical Year, which gives explanations of the Epistle and Gospel for the Sundays and many feast days. This is now in reprint as The Church's Year.

The Church Comfortable

Vatican II finished establishing the Church Comfortable. In fact, much Catholicism in the first half of the Twentieth Century had been reduced to Mass on Sunday, fish on Friday, and five dollars in the collection plate. There had been various appeals by the popes to the laity to work in harmony under the direction of their pastors for the good of the Church. The appeals went mostly unheeded. In fact, the pastors themselves ignored the reminders of the popes of their solemn responsibilities as pastors.

In Catechism we learn about the Communion of Saints, the Church Triumphant in Heaven, which we all should want to join, the Church Suffering in Purgatory for those who don't quite make Heaven and the Church Militant here on Earth. The Church Militant fights for the rights of God and His Church. They also fight the three enemies of salvation: the world, the flesh, and the Devil.

No, I have not added to the Communion of Saints. The Church Comfortable consists of those who do not live the Catholic way of life. I do not just mean those who commit the obvious gross sins, but also those who are lukewarm to the point of negligence. "I know thy works, that thou art neither cold nor hot. I would thou wert cold or hot. But because thou art lukewarm and neither cold nor hot, I will begin to vomit thee out of my mouth."[271] Those in the Church Comfortable may live the good life[272] here on Earth, but they will suffer eternally in Hell for their negligence and failure to do the will of God. "He who is content with saving himself and neglects the salvation of others cannot secure his own salvation."[273] Our responsibility is not just to save our own soul and the souls of our family. Our responsibility is also to our neighbor. Our neighbor is everyone

---

271 Apocalypse 3:15-16
272 As the world defines it.
273 <u>The Priest: His Dignity And Obligations</u>, Page: 131, Quoting Saint John Chrysostom

we meet in our life. One of the saints said that everyone we come in contact with should be better off for having known us. This means for a moment or for a lifetime.

By defining that a person can be saved in the practice of any religion whatsoever, the Vatican II Church eliminated the need for conversions, pretending all along that the need for conversion was desirable. Yes, the Vatican II Church will accept converts. But the Vatican II Church is not zealous in obtaining them. They believe all men ultimately will be saved.

One would think that the Traditionalists would be zealous fighters for converts. Yet, the Traditionalists are just about as zealous as the Vatican II church. They have found their comfortable niche where they obtain Mass on Sunday, eat fish on Friday, etc. They observe the externals of Catholicism as their ancestors did in the first half of the twentieth century, completely ignoring the Popes as their ancestors did. For Traditionalists, Catholicism consists of a Latin Mass, the Rosary, and the Scapular. However, the Sabbatine Privilege is too much effort for them. They content themselves with wearing the scapular. They also get some Traditionalist priest to commute the Little Office of the Blessed Virgin Mary to their daily Rosary.

Finally, the home alone group. This group rejects both the Vatican II Church and the Traditionalists. They content themselves with leaving off the illegitimate Latin Masses of the Traditionalists, but they retain the Rosary and the Scapular.

Speak to any of these groups of a crusade to spread Catholicism throughout the world and do you know what you will find instead? A crusade against your call for a crusade!

Catholic Action

Catholic Action is not a recent invention, it is a command of Jesus Christ, Himself!

> "Fear not therefore: better are you than many sparrows. Every one therefore that shall confess Me before men, I will also confess him before My Father who is in Heaven. But he that shall deny Me before men, I will also deny him before My Father who is in Heaven."[274]

Jesus obliges us to confess Him before men. Lest some think this is reserved to the clergy and religious, let us read what Saint John Chrysostom has to say:

> "He not only requires faith which is of the mind, but confession which is by the mouth, that He may exalt us higher, and raise us to a more open utterance, and a larger measure of love. For this is spoken not to the Apostles only. But to all."[275]

Saint Hillary amplifies this further:

> "This teaches us, that in what measure we have borne witness to Him upon Earth, in the same shall we have Him bear witness to us in Heaven before the face of God the Father. What more consoling thought can there be?"[276]

> "My brethren, if any of you err from the truth and one convert him: He must know that he who causeth a sinner to be converted from the error of

---

274 Matthew 10:32-33
275 <u>Catena Aurea</u>, Saint Thomas Aquinas, Page: 394
276 <u>Catena Aurea</u>, Saint Thomas Aquinas, Page: 393-394

his way shall save his soul from death and shall cover a multitude of sins."[277]

I would like to remind the Church Comfortable of what Jesus said:

> "For what is a man advantaged, if he gain the whole world and lose himself and cast away himself? For he that shall be ashamed of Me and of My words, of him the Son of Man shall be ashamed, when He shall come in His majesty and that of His Father and of the holy angels."[278]

We may be comfortable here on Earth, but our true home is Heaven. We must work so that all could come to Heaven.[279]

Saint Gregory Nanzianzen gives us some wise advice: "We must first be purified and then purify others; be filled with wisdom and make others wise; become light and give light; be near to God and lead others to Him; be sanctified and sanctify; guide others by the hand and counsel them with knowledge."[280] We purify ourselves by fighting against our vices and implanting virtue in their stead. But this is only the beginning.

The next step is to learn the truths of the Faith thoroughly as directed by the Popes. We should pay special attention to Saint Pius X in Acerbo Nimis. This we do by laying the foundation with the study of the Catechism. We then move forward from the Catechism to a good understanding of the current situation in the Church. The necessary solution must be implemented according to the Will of God.

---

277   James 5:19-20
278   Luke 9:25-6
279   We must work for the conversion of all to the Divine and Catholic Faith. This must not be confused with the heresy of universalism of Karol Wojtyla and the Vatican II Church that all **will** be saved. It is only through submission to God and His holy Church that we can be saved, and all are called to make this submission.
280   The Eternal Priesthood, Henry Edward CDardinal Manning, page 114

"Since it is a fact that in these days adults need instruction no less than the young, all pastors and those having the care of souls shall explain the catechism to the people in a plain and simple style adapted to the intelligence of their hearers. This shall be carried out on all holy days of obligation[281], at such time as is most convenient for the people, but not during the same hour when the children are instructed, and this instruction must be in addition to the usual homily on the Gospel which is delivered at the parochial Mass on Sundays and holy days. The catechetical instruction shall be based on the Catechism of the Council of Trent; and the matter is to be divided in such a way that in the space of four or five years, treatment will be given to the Apostles' Creed, the Sacraments, the Ten Commandments, the Lord's Prayer and the Precepts of the Church."[282]

---

281 The holydays of obligation are all Sundays, as well as certain major feast days, which vary by country. Please see your Catechism for more information
282 Acerbo nimis, Pope Saint Pius X, Paragraph 24

Chapter 8
What Is Most Important:
The Mass or the Faith?

"It is the Mass that matters." This motto was inspired by the Protestants, who attempted to destroy the Mass. Some have reasoned that if a Mass is valid, then it is pleasing to God. The Roman Catechism states: "Whoever will eat the Lamb outside of this house is profane: whoever is not in the Ark of Noah shall perish in the flood."[283]

At the time of the Protestant Reformation, the Reformers knew well that by destroying the Mass they could separate souls from the Church. As Adrian Fortescue wrote in the Catholic Encyclopedia: "The words of the Reformers, 'It is the Mass that matters' was true."[284] Fortescue explained that all King Henry VIII needed to do was outlaw the Mass; "a general denial of the whole system of Catholic dogma was unnecessary."[285] (Unaware it was a Protestant slogan, Catholics used this phrase in the early days following the abolition of the Tridentine.) The Catholics emblazoned those words on the banner of their opposition: "It is the Mass that matters." But while Fortescue observed that "the Mass is the central feature of the Catholic religion," he said something else even more important. This was something overlooked by those early champions of the Tridentine Mass who were eager to preserve the liturgy.

"As union with Rome is the bond between Catholics, so is our common share in this, the most venerable rite in Christendom, the witness and safeguard of that bond."[286] The Mass, then, is the external expression of our union with Rome, our obedience to and reverence for the papacy. By itself, it is NOT the bond that guarantees unity, only its safeguard. This is

---
283   Catechism of the Council of Trent, Page: 74
284   Catholic Encyclopedia, Volume 9, Page: 800
285   Catholic Encyclopedia, Volume 9, Page: 800
286   Catholic Encyclopedia, Volume 9, Page: 800

the teaching of Pope Pius XII in Mystici Corporis, where the Pope stated: "By means of the Eucharistic Sacrifice, Christ Our Lord willed to give to the faithful a striking manifestation of our union among ourselves and with our Divine Head...The Sacrament of the Eucharist is itself a striking and wonderful figure of the unity of the Church..."[287] When Montini abolished the true Mass, he effectively announced that the safeguard of that unity was no longer needed.

The Reformers and those evil men working behind the scenes to destroy the Church learned a valuable lesson. They reversed the order necessary to accomplish their ultimate goal. Destroying the Mass alone was not the answer, although, certainly it was the first step in their graduated plan to eventually overthrow the Holy See. It is important to remember that irregularities in the liturgy cropped up worldwide long before Pope Pius XII issued Mediator Dei, (November 30, 1947). When the problem continued, Pope Pius XII extended Canon 1, paragraph 2 of the Oriental Code of Canon Law to the Universal Church. That law states: "Patriarchs, Archbishops and other Ordinaries should zealously care for the faithful protection and the accurate observance of their rite, nor are they to permit or to tolerate any change in the rite."[288] This should be seen in its true light by those so zealous to preserve the Mass. Without Canon Law and the power of the Holy See to interpret it, add to or subtract from it, the Mass is vulnerable to attack and perversion. Those wishing to sidestep Canon Law in other matters need to realize that without these laws the integrity of the Church cannot be preserved. The revision of the Code of Canon Law by Wojtyla as Antipope John Paul II the Great Deceiver in 1983 was scarcely a coincidence.

Only the Pope can protect the Mass; the Mass by itself cannot constitute or represent the unbroken totality of Church unity. The papacy was the guarantor of the existence of the Holy Sacrifice from the beginning. The papacy's (apparent)

---

287 Mystici Corporis, Pope Pius XII, Paragrah 82
288 Canon Law Digest, Volume 5, Page: 7

cessation was only an indicator of the Church's (apparent) demise.[289] Pope Saint Pius X gave evidence of this essential connection in his encyclical, <u>Pascendi Dominici Gregis</u>. Teaching against the errors of vital permanence and the collective conscience, he sternly reminded Catholics that "the triple authority in the Church (is): disciplinary, dogmatic, and liturgical." While the Modernists taught that the Church is obliged to join the State in adopting "democratic forms of procedure," Pope Saint Pius X defined as "mad (those) who think that the sense of liberty now flourishing," could ever cause the Church to change Her God-given form of government or teaching. The Church, image of the Trinity Itself cannot change what God has ordained. What the faithful saw was exactly the opposite of what they think they perceived. The authority Montini arrogated did not exist: it derived from a diabolic source. Antipope Paul VI, as Pope Leo XIII predicted in his long version of the Saint Michael's Prayer, was "the abominable impiety" in the Holy Place. Antipope Paul VI pretended to be the voice of God. He revealed his true identity in abolishing the Latin Tridentine Mass. Montini was not pope — he was the antithesis of all that was holy.

The Devil hates the Papacy. Jesus founded His Church upon a Rock (Petrus): "And I say to thee: That thou art Peter; and upon this rock I will build my church, and the gates of Hell shall not prevail against it."[290] The Devil knows that the only way to destroy the Church is to destroy the Papacy.[291]

"For the mystery of iniquity already worketh, only that he who now holdeth do hold, until he be taken out of the way."[292] Let us see what this means. Concerning this quote from Saint Paul, Fr. Berry writes: "The words of Saint Paul to the

---

289   We know that the Church cannot cease to exist, but there will be an unprecedented crisis in history, when it can appear to have ceased to exist to most of the world.
290   Matthew 16:18
291   It is infallible that the Church cannot be destroyed, but it can be severely crippled.
292   II Thessalonians 2:7

Thessalonians may be a reference to the papacy as the obstacle to the coming of Antichrist."²⁹³ Let us apply this to our situation. By attempting to elect the heretic Angelo Roncalli as pope in October 1958, the cardinals gave us an antipope instead of giving us a pope.

What solution was pursued to end the confusion of the Western Schism? First, we had one pope. Then, the cardinals said they were coerced. They left Rome and elected a second claimant. The Council of Pisa deposed the claimant from each of the two lines and elected a third. This is beyond the authority of a Council. Finally, the Council of Constance deposed Antipope John XXIII who had called it. Pope Gregory XII resigned in favor of a new election. Then, the Council deposed the final claimant.²⁹⁴ This being done, the Papacy was certainly vacant. The Council proceeded to elect Pope Martin V.

In our time it can be certainly demonstrated that the papacy became vacant on October 9, 1958. The apparent elections of 1958, 1963, 1978 and 2005 are also certainly invalid. Each man apparently elected in all five cases was a heretic prior to his election. In the cases of the 1963 and 1978 elections there are other irregularities. The solution to the crisis is to accept or elect a pope who can set all else back in proper order.²⁹⁵

---

293   The Apocalypse of St. John, Page: 121
294   A Council can depose an Antipope, but not the true Pope because the Pope is above a Council.
295   It must be noted that all of the men claiming to be Cardinals will assemble shortly to elect a successor to Benedict XVI. They are heretics. Therefore they have resigned the office of Cardinal.

Chapter 9
The Solution?

"Indeed we declare, say, pronounce, and define that it is altogether necessary to salvation for every human creature to be subject to the Roman Pontiff."[296]

Many do not realize that Archbishop Peter Martin Ngo-Dihn Thuc called for the election of a Pope in his Declaration in 1982. This was discussed in several meetings by the Thuc Bishops in 1982 and in 1983. In January of 1983, Archbishop Thuc and all of his Bishops with the exception of Bishop Guerard des Lauriers assembled to discuss this matter and prepare for the election of a Pope, **so that the Church of Rome can endure** as Thuc had declared a year before in 1982. A small group of Thuc Bishops assembled a Papal Election in 1994, as will be considered ahead

---

[296]   The Sources Of Catholic Dogma, # 469, Page: 187

Pope Gregory XVII?

Which one? Today there are two men who claimed to be Pope Gregory XVII. There is a third man that some claim was Pope Gregory XVII. The first two can be dismissed because they were not elected, but appointed by some alleged vision.[297] However, the claim for the third Gregory should be addressed briefly.

The Siri Theory - It was originally claimed that Cardinal Siri was elected in 1963 and both 1978 conclaves, but preventing from either accepting or rejecting the election thus becoming a *pope-elect.* [298] After his death, it was then claimed that he was also elected in 1958 and accepted. The hopes of the Siri proponents did not end with his death on May 2, 1989. It has been claimed that either he appointed secret cardinals, or that he appointed a successor that reigns in secret. There is evidence that there was confusion in 1958. Someone was apparently elected in 1958 and white smoke indeed went up, but...

We can summarize the Siri claim. First of all, Cardinal Siri never claimed to be Pope. Secondly, Siri publicly accepted, by his silence, men whom he knew to be antipopes. These men are: John XXIII, Paul VI, John Paul I and John Paul II.[299] Siri interceded with Antipope Paul VI on behalf of Lefebvre. The reason Siri did this was to obtain an audience for Lefebvre with Antipope Paul VI. Siri participated in Vatican II, and instituted the Novus Ordo Missae, and the accompanying new sacramental rites in his diocese of Genoa. This was something no true pope could do. We must conclude that Siri was not pope.

---

297   One lived in Palmar de Troya, Spain and was ordained and consecrated by Archbishop Ngo-Dihn Thuc. The other in St. Jovite, Canada.
298   A man is considered a pope-elect, the moment he receives the required votes until he expresses his acceptance or rejection of the Papal Election.
299   If Siri was Pope, then he would **know** these men were Antipopes.

Papal Claimants

There are more claimants to the papacy today than at any other time in history, a fact Antipope Benedict XVI and the false Vatican does not want you to know. We have mentioned three Gregorys XVII. There are more papal claimants that are appointed by alleged apparitions. There have been four Papal Elections held. The first on July 16, 1990, the second in 1994, the third on October 28, 1998 and the fourth on March 24, 2006.[300]

Pope Benedict XIV says: "today it is evident that Urban VI and his successors were legitimate Pontiffs."[301] Urban VI was the first elected at the time of the Western Schism. A second claimant was elected by the same Cardinals six months later. A third line started at the Council of Pisa, which no one holds to be legitimate. Forty years after the election of Urban VI, his successor, the true Pope, Gregory XII, resigned in favor of a new election at the Council of Constance. This helps establish the principle that the first in time is the first in right.

This can be further demonstrated. The 1994, 1998 and 2006 elections did not address the previous election in 1990. The 1990 election addressed all of the claimants prior to its commencement. Many of the participants in the 1994 and 1998 elections possessed the book Will the Catholic Church Survive the Twentieth Century?. This book was written to call for a Papal Election in 1990.

We must recall that the Holy Ghost oversees the election

---

300   David Bawden as Pope Michael in 1990
Victor Von Pentz as Pope Linus II in 1995
Lucian Pulvermacher as Pope Pius XIII in 1998
Oscar Michaeli as Leo XIV
Von Pentz has virtually resigned. Pulvermacher has died and his group is preparing for an internet email election for the fall of 2010. Michaeli died and was succeeded by Luan Batista Bonetti. Who took the name Innocent XIV. Bonetti resigned and was succeeded by Alexanger Greico, who took the name of Alexander IX. Reports are Greico has resigned into a vacuum.
301   Studies In Church History, Page: 539

of a Pope, and God grants the Pope authority the moment he is elected, no matter how irregular the election may have been. Recall that all that is required for a man to be validly elected Pope is that he be a reasonable Catholic man. That is he must be baptized, have the use of reason and be a member of the Catholic Church, therefore heretics, apostates and schismatics cannot become Pope.

The Second Council of Lyons states: "How grave are the losses resulting from a prolonged vacancy, and how full of dangers it is to the Roman Church, is shown by prudent consideration of the past."[302]

The Catholic Church is "the assembly of believers in Christ, under the obedience to the successors of Saint Peter."[303]

---

302   Disciplinary Decrees of the General Council, Page: 331
303   A Systematic Study of the Catholic Religion, Page: 61

Chapter 10
Mission of the Catholic Church

"As the Father has sent Me, I also send you",[304] Jesus said to the Apostles. Saint Paul asks,

> "How then shall they call on him in whom they have not believed? Or how shall they believe him of whom they have not heard? And how shall they hear without a preacher? And how shall they preach unless they be sent, as it is written: How beautiful are the feet of them that preach the gospel of peace, of them that bring glad tidings of good things?"[305]

Jesus sent the Apostles as a group into the world to teach in His Name.

> "Going therefore, teach ye all nations: baptizing them in the name of the Father and of the Son and of the Holy Ghost. Teaching them to observe all things whatsoever I have commanded you. And behold I am with you all days, even to the consummation of the world."[306]

Note well, that whenever Jesus gave a power to the Apostles, Peter was there as their head. The only time an Apostle was missing was after the Resurrection, when Jesus said: "Whose sins you shall forgive, they are forgiven them: and whose sins you shall retain, they are retained."[307] Thomas was not there. So, how did Doubting Thomas receive the authority

---
304 John 20:21
305 Romans 10:14-15
      tthew 28:19-20
      n 20:21

to forgive sins? Sacred Scripture does not tell us. Who sent Thomas? Either Jesus gave him authority directly or more like Peter as the Vicar of Jesus Christ transmitted this authority himself.

Msgr. Charles Journet states:

> Bellarmine replies that the apostolate carried with it only the right to preach and a delegated jurisdictional power of wide extension but including neither the power of order nor the episcopate. It is be insisted that on this view bishops would not be successors of the Apostles, he replies that the bishops are certainly successors of the Apostles, not however because the apostolate included the episcopate, but because the Apostles were, additionally, bishops-that they were even the first bishops of the Church although they were ordained by Peter and not by Christ.[308]

Under this proposition, Jesus Christ consecrated Peter as a Bishop, who in turn consecrated the rest of the Apostles. We know that it is a matter of Faith that Jesus ordained the Apostles priests at the Last Supper. If this is true, it shows more profoundly how all power in the Catholic Church flows from Jesus through the Vicar of Jesus Christ.

In Acts we find that Peter presided over the election of Mathias to replace Judas, who had apostatized. Henry Cardinal Manning states:

> "Saint Optatus says that for the good of unity Blessed Peter was preferred before all the Apostles, and alone received the keys of the kingdom of Heaven, to communicate them to the others. But the power of binding and loosing, which, depending on the power of the keys,

---
308   The Church of the Word Incarnate, pages 384-5

> signifies ecclesiastical jurisdiction, though it was given by Christ Himself to the other Apostles, was not, however, given to any of them singly, as to Saint Peter but in common and collectively with Peter, who was also with the others when Christ said, 'Whatsoever you shall bind on Earth,' etc., that all may understand that Bishops, the successors of the Apostles, can do nothing except in unity with Peter and with the successors of Peter"[309]

We must recall that the authority given to the Apostles was given to them in union with Peter, but that certain powers were given to Peter alone without the rest of the Apostles receiving that power. The first of these is the power of the keys, given in Matthew 16. The two keys are that of government and science, according to Cardinal Manning, who is following the traditional teaching of the Catholic Church.[310]

The dogma of the infallibility of the Pope flows from the key of doctrine, which is confirmed by Jesus, when He said to Saint Peter: "And the Lord said: Simon, Simon, behold Satan hath desired to have you, that he may sift you as wheat. But I have prayed for thee, that thy faith fail not: and thou, being once converted, confirm thy brethren."[311] Fr. O'Reilly in his <u>Relations of the Church to Society</u> states:

> "The need of the people is sufficiently provided for in this respect, if there be a living authority in the Church that presides over all religious teaching, an authority on which all local teacher depend, and are known to depend, and which affords a public standard of doctrine whereby deviations on the part of individual pastors would be at once

---

309   <u>The Pastoral Office</u>, Page: 9
310   <u>Pastoral Office</u>, Page: 19
311   Luke 22:31-32

discovered."³¹²

In several places in his work he refers to the necessity of a single living person, who can teach infallibly in the Name of Jesus Christ, and that person is the Pope, the Vicar of Jesus Christ.

Fr. O'Reilly also tells us why we need a Pope: "But questions have arisen on which the integrity of Catholic doctrine demanded a prompt decision..."³¹³ Bishops can give a theological opinion, but always important matters were referred to Rome, that is to the decision of the Pope. And today, there are many questions that have arisen since Vatican II, which need resolution. A resolution which only a living Pope can give! We must conclude that the Pope is necessary to ensure sound doctrine. What would happen if the Papacy were to remain vacant for a long time? The prophesy of Saint Paul would come true:

> "For there shall be a time when they will not endure sound doctrine but, according to their own desires, they will heap to themselves teachers having itching ears. And will indeed turn away their hearing from the truth, but will be turned unto fables."³¹⁴

When they "hap to themselves", they are granting these teachers authority over them, which is not Catholic. Authority in the Catholic Church comes from God through the Vicar of Jesus Christ, the Pope to the Bishops of the various dioceses. These Bishops in turn appoint priests to teach and govern the faithful in the various parishes. Protestants appoint their own preachers and can as easily dismiss them. This practice has been condemned by the Church.

---

312 Relations of the Church to Society, Page: 38
313 Relations of the Church to Society, Page: 36
314 II Timothy 4:3-4

In fact, although we know there was a Pope during the Western Schism, the scandal of the schism opened the door for the doctrines, which led a century later to the Protestant Revolt. Father Edmund James O'Reilly, wrote: "...not that an interregnum covering the whole period"[315] (of the Western Schism) "would have been impossible or inconsistent with the promises of Christ, for this is by no means manifest." If the confusion of several claimants to the Papacy over forty years can cause such confusion, consider a vacancy with an antipope only!

The Catholic Church is one and we read earlier in the <u>Roman Catechism</u>: "That this visible head is necessary to establish and preserve unity in the Church is the unanimous accord of the Fathers..."[316] A living, breathing Pope is necessary at the head of the Apostolic College in order to insure unity, as Pope Leo XIII stated: "But the Episcopal order is rightly judged to be in communion with Peter, as Christ commanded, if it be subject to and obeys Peter; otherwise it necessarily becomes a lawless and disorderly crowd."[317] Bishops who are not in visible union with a living Pope become a disorderly crowd and are blown about by every wind of doctrine and thus are not truly Apostolic, for Apostolicity requires three things, doctrine and mission, to which are attached the Order of Bishop. The Office of Bishop cannot be possessed without union with the Pope, who alone has the keys of doctrine and government.

The key of government is essential to good order in the Catholic Church, and by divine institution, the Church is a monarchy established upon the Bishop of Rome, who is also Vicar of Jesus Christ.[318] The Pope by divine institution is

---

315 "This schism was only material, not formal; for though there was great practical difficulty in recognizing the rightful claimant, the principle of obedience to the legitimate pontiff was not denied." (<u>A Systematic Study Of The Catholic Religion</u>, Page: 76)
316 <u>Catechism of the Council of Trent</u>, Page: 74
317 <u>Satis Cognitum</u>, Pope Leo XIII, Paragraph 15
318 The Bishop of Rome is the Pope, and the Pope is Bishop of Rome, even if he never physically sets foot in Rome itself, as the theologians and

commissioned by Jesus to feed the lambs and the sheep.[319] Pope Benedict XIV states: "The care of both the lambs of the Lord's flock (who are the people scattered through the entire world) and of the sheep (the bishops who act as tender parents of the lambs) is entrusted to the Pope."[320] Cardinals Manning says:

> "The potestas clavium or the power of the keys, and the potestas regiminis or the power of government, according to Ballerini, are equivalent. The signification of the key of David as the government, or throne, promised to the Messias, is sufficient proof. This we have already seen in the first and second chapters. Now, Saint Gregory the Great says: 'To all who know the Gospel it is plain that by the voice of our Lord the care of the whole Church was committed to Saint Peter, head of all the Apostles....To him it is said: 'Thou art Peter...and to thee will I give the keys of the kingdom of Heaven' etc. See, he receives the keys of the heavenly kingdom; the power of binding and loosing is given to him, the care and primacy of the whole Church is committed to him.'"[321]

Sacred Scripture talks in several places about the Key of David,[322] which will be given to Jesus Christ and by Him to Saint Peter and his successors, who will reign until the end of time.

> "And I say to thee: That thou art Peter; and upon this rock I will build my church, and the gates of Hell shall not prevail against it. And I will give to

---
history prove.
319   John 21:15-16
320   <u>Ubi Primum</u>, Pope Benedict XI, 3 December 1740
321   <u>The Pastoral Office</u>, Page: 81
322   Apocalypse 3:7 & Isaias 22:22

thee the keys of the kingdom of Heaven. And whatsoever thou shalt bind upon Earth, it shall be bound also in Heaven: and whatsoever thou shalt loose on Earth, it shall be loosed also in Heaven."[323]

The keys were given only to Peter and not to the rest, so the rest of the clergy, Bishops, priests and other clerics must receive their key directly or indirectly from the Pope. The Pope regulates the manner of electing or appointing Bishops and under the current law directly appoints the Bishops. Even when Bishops were elected, they could not assume their office until their appointment was confirmed by the Pope. The current law provides that a man receives the Office of Bishop, when he has been appointed and presents the letters of appointment to the officials of the diocese, even before he has been consecrated to the Order of Bishop. The keys of doctrine and government are handed on to him for his diocese by the Pope, which entitles him to receive the Order of Bishop.

We have seen how Bishops are sent and become Apostolic, how is the Pope sent? The Pope is sent by election, and the moment a man accepts election as Pope, he receives the keys of doctrine and government with the right to receive the Order of Priest and of Bishop, if he does not previously possess them. Note well that the Papacy is not handed on by the laying on of hands, nor is the Office of Bishop. This is the transmission of the Order of Bishop not the Office of Bishop. These are two distinct things, the Order and Office of Bishop. All who hold the Office of Bishop should also possess the Order of Bishop, but in history some men have held the Office without the Order. What has happened is that Traditionalist men who wish to reign over their own private jurisdiction have confused the Order and Office of Bishop, holding that both are conferred by the laying on of hands. The principle is that there should be one shepherd over each diocese, that is one Bishop. If there are several Bishops in the same diocese, all are subject to the Bishop or

---

323   Matthew 16:18-19

Shepherd of the diocese, just as that Bishop is subject to the Pope. All is in an orderly hierarchy, which depends for its unity and Catholicity upon a single head to rule the Church, which is the Pope, the Vicar of Jesus Christ, the invisible Head of the Church.

> "Indeed we declare, say, pronounce, and define that it is altogether necessary to salvation for every human creature to be subject to the Roman Pontiff."[324]

We can draw the logical conclusion that it is also necessary for salvation to have a living Pope to be subject to. The Second Council of Lyons states: "How grave are the losses resulting from a prolonged vacancy, and how full of dangers it is to the Roman Church, is shown by prudent consideration of the past." This Council was one of those called to end the problem of year long vacancies in the Papacy. Canon Law provides: "The laity has the right to receive from the clergy the spiritual goods and especially the necessary means of salvation, according to the rules of ecclesiastical discipline."[325] Can't we reason, then, that the clergy are obliged to provide us with a Pope?

Of course, most vacancies proceed smoothly to an election, but the vacancy that began on October 9th, 1958 is extraordinary in that the ordinary electors all ceased to exist by the end of Vatican II with several possible exceptions who were in prison and unable to attend Vatican II. By 1990 all were dead. Thus the Church was obliged to provide for the election of a Pope in an extraordinary manner. Theologians and Canonists debate on the exact manner the Church would proceed in such a case, but all are agreed that under the Natural Law, the Universal Church can supply herself with a Pope, and thus no matter how the Church proceeds during such a vacancy, it

---

324   Unam Sanctam, Pope Boniface VIII
325   A Practical Commentary On The Code Of Canon Law, Volume 1, Canon 682, Page: 341

would be valid and thus the man elected Pope would truly be Pope.

The Catholic Church is a perfect society as Pope Leo XIII states in <u>Satis Cognitum</u>.[326] As a prefect society, the Church always has the means of providing herself with a head. The State is also a perfect society, which is why the government always has a means of providing itself with the necessary officers to govern, even in an emergency. Perfect societies have certain abilities under the Natural Law, which are given by Almighty God so they can discharge their responsibilities, for all authority comes from Almighty God. If people intervene in any manner, it is to designate the person whom God will grant the authority to, thus the Pope does not receive his authority from the people who elect him, but from Almighty God. All the electors do is designate the person God grants the authority to as we pray in the Church: "O God, the Pastor and Ruler of all the faithful, look favorably upon Thy servant N, Whom Thou hast been pleased to appoint as shepherd of Thy Church..."[327]

Saint Anthony Mary Claret says: "He who is not with Peter is not with the Church, and he who leaves the Ark will perish in the time of the flood." Pope Leo XIII stated in <u>Satis Cognitum</u>:

> "Remember and understand well that where Peter is, there is the Church; that those who refuse to associate in communion with the Chair of Peter belong to Antichrist, not to Christ. He who would separate himself from the Roman Pontiff has no further bond with Christ."[328]

And all should be familiar with Saint Ambrose: "Where Peter is, there is the Church." And so, where is Peter?

---

326   <u>Satis Cognitum</u>, Pope Leo XIII, "For this reason we find it called in Holy Writ by names indicating a perfect society."
327   <u>Saint Pius X Daily Missal</u>, Page: 931
328   <u>Satis Cognitum</u>, Pope Leo XIII, June 29, 1896

Habemus Papam

> "And to the angel of the church of Philadelphia write: These things saith the Holy One and the true one, he that hath the key of David, he that openeth and no man shutteth, shutteth and no man openeth."[329]

Allow me to introduce myself. I am David Bawden. I was elected Pope on July 16, 1990, taking the name of Michael. I have waited until now to introduce myself. This is because many dismiss my claim without considering the basis upon which I make this claim.

"Indeed we declare, say, pronounce, and define that it is altogether necessary to salvation for every human creature to be subject to the Roman Pontiff."[330]

It was not so much this infallible teaching of the Catholic Church that convinced me of my responsibility to work for a papal election on September 8, 1987. Rather it was the infallible teaching of the Vatican Council[331] that Saint Peter will have a perpetual line of successors in the Papacy that prompted my actions.

> "If anyone then says that it is not from the institution of Christ the Lord Himself, or by divine right that the blessed Peter has perpetual successors in the primacy over the universal Church, or that the Roman Pontiff is not the successor of the blessed Peter in the same primacy, let him be anathema."[332]

---

329 Apocalypse 3:7
330 Unam Sanctam, Pope Boniface VIII
331 There is only one Vatican Council. It was held in 1869-79. Vatican II is not a Catholic Council.
332 The Sources Of Catholic Dogma, # 1825, Page: 453

The solution to the current Church crisis was undertaken by a handful of Catholics in July 1990. Despite my strong desire to the contrary, I was elected Pope and chose the name Michael on July 16, 1990.

"For many are called but few chosen."[333] Actually, many were called. The book, <u>Will the Catholic Church Survive the Twentieth Century?</u> was sent to sede vacantists throughout the world at no little effort. This includes all of the Thuc-line Bishops and all sede vacantist chapels, which would include most of the sede vacantists priests. In fact, prior to its publication, much effort was put forth to encourage sede vacantists to end the vacancy in the papacy as the only solution to our problems. In 1989, and early 1990, some showed interest. Then they all began to make excuses why they did not want a papal election now. When, may we ask, would be a good time? The papacy had been vacant for three decades already. The second longest interregnum was ended with force.[334] The cardinals had assembled. Instead of electing a pope they were making merry. The laity after over two years became frustrated with the cardinals. The laity boarded up the doors and windows. The laity cut the cardinals' rations to bread and water. When this did not work, the laity removed the roof. Soon the cardinals came in out of the rain. We can see what three decades of delay has wrought! Vatican II did not commence until five years after the vacancy began. The Novus Ordo was not instituted until the second decade of the vacancy. The vacancy has seen many other peripheral scandals. One of the many scandals being well publicized is the pedophile scandal. These scandals, serious as they are, pale in comparison to the heresies which those claiming to be Catholic happily believe. Above the Second Council of Lyons told us how dangerous a prolonged vacancy is in the Papacy.

"Truth, as the proverb says, is a very beautiful

---

333   Matthew 20:16
334   1268-1271 A.D.

mother, but she usually bears a very ugly daughter; Hatred. Saint John (the Baptist) experienced that speaking the truth very often arouses hatred and enmity against the speaker. Let us learn from him to speak the truth always, when responsibility requires it, even if it brings upon us the greatest misfortunes, for, if with Saint John we patiently bear persecution, with Saint John we shall become martyrs for truth."[335]

We fully expect this book to produce love in some and hatred from others. The Abbess Maria Steiner prophesied: "The people will be like the Christians of the primitive Church."[336] We will imitate the zealousness of the early Christians and we may have to follow them to holy martyrdom.

---

335   Explanation of the Epistles and Gospels for the Sundays, Holydays, and Festivals throughout the Ecclesiastical Year to which are added the Lives of Many Saints, Pages: 23-24
336   The Prophets And Our Times, Page: 200

Chapter 11
An Urgent Appeal

On the day of judgment, Jesus will come to the place where you have just died according to Saint John Eudes. He will ask you what you did with the information you just read above. Divine Providence has placed this book in your hands, and Almighty God desires you to do something with it. If you agree, then your course is clear, join with Jesus Christ and His vicar on Earth in the Ark of Salvation and carry forward. If you disagree, then you have a responsibility to prove where the reasoning above contradicts the Divine and Catholic Faith. Jesus says: "He that is not with me is against Me."[337] Now many will read this out of curiosity and stay in their easy chair and do nothing. These want to be members of the Church Comfortable. To these, Jesus said: "He who gathereth not with Me, scattereth."[338] On the **Day of Judgment (Dies Irae)**[339] those who agree will more likely be saved, and even those who disagree and do something about it have a chance to be saved, but the broadminded and indifferent have no chance of salvation. In Apocalypse we are warned: "I know thy works, that thou art neither cold nor hot. I would thou wert cold or hot. But because thou art lukewarm and neither cold nor hot, I will begin to vomit thee out of my mouth."[340]

We must ask ourselves why God placed this book in our hands now and what He expects us to do about it. This book will raise up two classes of warriors. Those who fight with Jesus for the exaltation of the Catholic Church and those who fight against the Catholic Church, which army will you join?

---

337 Matthew 12:30
338 Matthew 12:30
339 "Day of Wrath." (A Catholic Dictionary, Page: 147)
340 Apocalypse 3:15-16

More Information

In order to join with the Catholic Church, Pope Michael requires all to be baptized and submit proof of Baptism to his office in exile at:

Vatican In Exile
Box 74
Delia, KS 66418-9792
USA

The Pope also requires the simple Profession of Faith of Pope Michael found after this short section. This needs to be signed and mailed in to the Pope. It is recommended to submit a brief story of your religious history. Clergy, who wish to join may begin with the above. Those who wish to be admitted to the clergy in the Church will be requested to meet with the Pope personally before beginning their public function as clergy. Clergy will also make the Oath Against the Errors of Modernism and the Profession of Faith of the Council of Trent.

The Pope fully understands this is a time of confusion and many have been deceived and been members of this or that sect, some of which are described above. Saint Augustine reminds us that to err is human, and the Pope fully realizes this and wishes to welcome all into the Catholic Church and to help all on the road to salvation.

"But to willfully remain in error is Satanic"
- Saint Augustine

Professions of Faith

Profession of Faith Prescribed by Pope Michael

I believe in God, the Father Almighty, Creator of Heaven and Earth, and in Jesus Christ His only Son, Our Lord; Who was conceived by the Holy Ghost, born of the Virgin Mary, suffered under Pontius Pilate, was crucified, died and was buried: He descended into Hell; the third day he arose again from the dead; He ascended into Heaven; sitteth at the right hand of God the Father almighty: from thence He shall come to judge the living and the dead. I believe in the Holy Ghost, the holy Catholic Church, the communion of Saints, the forgiveness of sins, the resurrection of the body and life everlasting.

I renounce Satan, and all his works, and all his allurements.

I accept everything the holy, Catholic and Apostolic Church teaches and believes, as She teaches and believes them, especially those things which are de fide; of faith.

I reject each and every error, which the One, Holy, Catholic and Apostolic Church rejects, as She rejects and condemns them, without reservation. Furthermore, I declare anathema every heresy against the One Holy Catholic Apostolic Church, and likewise whosoever has honored or believes any writings beyond those which the One Holy Catholic Apostolic Church accepts ought to be held on the authority, or any who have venerated them. Whatever the One Holy Catholic Apostolic Church believes and praises, I also believe and praise, and whoever they declare anathema, I declare anathema.[341]

I promise obedience to the infallible Supreme Pontiff of the Apostolic See and to his canonically elected successor under the testimony of Christ, affirming what the holy and universal Church affirms and condemning what she condemns.[342] I accept

---

341   The Sources Of Catholic Dogma, # 349, Page: 142
342   The Sources Of Catholic Dogma, # 357, Page: 145

the authority of the Roman Pontiff, that when he shall decide a matter it is forever closed. I accept the laws of the Church as the Church interprets them and reject any interpretation that contradicts the interpretation of the Church. I submit fully to Pope Michael I, Successor of Saint Peter.

Explanation of the Profession of Faith Prescribed by Pope Michael

This Profession of Faith was compiled from previous Professions of Faith as noted in the notes above. We have numbered this so that it may be taken section at a time.

This begins with the Apostles Creed, the core of the Catholic Faith. The next lines were inspired by the Formula prescribe for all the cities of the Eastern Church at the Lateran Council in 1102,[343] affirming what the holy and universal Church affirms and condemning what she condemns.

"Likewise, all other things I accept and profess, which the Holy Roman Church accepts and professes, and I likewise condemn, reject, and anathematize, at the same time all contrary things, both schisms and heresies, which have been condemned by the same Church."[344] The part in the Profession is taken from the Symbol of Faith of Pope Saint Leo IX, April 13, 1053.

"I promise and swear true obedience to the Roman Pontiff, the successor of Blessed Peter, the prince of the Apostles and the vicar of Jesus Christ."[345] This is from the Profession of Faith prescribed for the Orientals on March 16, 1743 by Pope Benedict XIV in the Constitution Nuper ad nos. The Profession was inspired by the Lateran Council in a formula prescribed for the Eastern Church: "I declare anathema every heresy and especially that one which disturbs the present Church, which teaches and declares that excommunication is to be despised and that the restrictions of the Church are to be cast aside. Moreover, I promise obedience to Paschal, the supreme Pontiff of the Apostolic See, and to his successors under the testimony of Christ and the Church, affirming what the holy and universal Church affirms and condemning what she condemns."[346]

343	The Sources Of Catholic Dogma, # 357, Page: 145	
344	The Sources Of Catholic Dogma, # 1473, Page: 360	
345	The Sources Of Catholic Dogma, # 1473, Page: 360	
346	The Sources Of Catholic Dogma, # 357, Page: 145	

Profession of Faith of Trent

I, _____, with firm faith believe and profess all and everything which is contained in the creed of faith, which the holy Roman Church uses; namely: I believe in one God, the Father Almighty, maker of Heaven and Earth, and of all things visible and invisible; and in one Lord Jesus Christ, the only-begotten Son of God, born of the Father before all ages; God from God, light from light, true God from true God; begotten not made, of one substance with the Father; through whom all things were made; who for us men and for our salvation came down from Heaven, and was made incarnate by the Holy Ghost of the Virgin Mary, and was made man. He was crucified also for us under Pontius Pilate, died, and was buried; and He rose again the third day according to the Scriptures, and ascended into Heaven; He sits at the right hand of the Father, and He shall come again in glory to judge the living and the dead, and of His kingdom there will be no end. And I believe in the Holy Ghost, the Lord, and giver of life, who proceeds from the Father and the Son; who equally with the Father and the Son is adored and glorified; who spoke through the prophets. And I believe that there is One, Holy, Catholic, and Apostolic Church. I confess one baptism for the remission of sins; and I hope for the resurrection of the dead, and the life of the world to come. Amen."[347]

"I resolutely accept and embrace the apostolic and ecclesiastical traditions and the other practices and regulations of that same Church. In like manner I accept Sacred Scripture according to the meaning which has been held by holy Mother Church and which she now holds. It is her prerogative to pass judgment on the true meaning and interpretation of Sacred Scripture. And I will never accept or interpret it in a manner different from the unanimous agreement of the Fathers."[348]

"I also acknowledge that there are truly and properly seven Sacraments of the New Law, instituted by Jesus Christ our

---

347   The Sources Of Catholic Dogma, # 994, Page: 302
348   The Sources Of Catholic Dogma, # 995, Page: 303

Lord, and that they are necessary for the salvation of the human race, although it is not necessary for each individual to receive them all. I acknowledge that the seven Sacraments are: Baptism, Confirmation, Holy Eucharist, Penance, Extreme Unction, Holy Orders, and Matrimony; and that they confer grace; and that of the seven, Baptism, Confirmation, and Holy Orders cannot be repeated without committing a sacrilege. I also accept and acknowledge the customary and approved rites of the Catholic Church in the solemn administration of these Sacraments. I embrace and accept each and every article on original sin and justification declared and defined in the most holy Council of Trent."[349]

"I likewise profess that in the Mass a true, proper and propitiatory sacrifice is offered to God on behalf of the living and the dead, and that the Body and Blood together with the soul and divinity of our Lord Jesus Christ is truly, really, and substantially present in the most holy sacrament of the Eucharist, and that there is a change of the whole substance of the bread into the Body, and of the whole substance of the wine into Blood; and this change the Catholic Church calls transubstantiation. I also profess that the whole and entire Christ and a true sacrament is received under each separate species."[350]

"I firmly hold that there is a purgatory, and that the souls detained there are helped by the prayers of the faithful. I likewise hold that the saints reigning together with Christ should be honored and invoked, that they offer prayers to God on our behalf, and that their relics should be venerated. I firmly assert that images of Christ, of the Mother of God ever Virgin, and of the other saints should be owned and kept, and that due honor and veneration should be given to them. I affirm that the power of indulgences was left in the keeping of the Church by Christ, and that the use of indulgences is very beneficial to

---

349   The Sources Of Catholic Dogma, # 996, Page: 303
350   The Sources Of Catholic Dogma, # 997, Page: 303

Christians."[351]

"I acknowledge the Holy, Catholic, and Apostolic Roman Church as the mother and teacher of all churches; and I promise and swear true obedience to the Roman Pontiff, vicar of Christ and successor of Blessed Peter, Prince of the Apostles."[352]

"I unhesitatingly accept and profess all the doctrines (especially those concerning the primacy of the Roman Pontiff and his infallible teaching authority), handed down, defined and explained by the sacred canons and the ecumenical councils and especially those of this most holy Council of Trent (and by the ecumenical Vatican Council). And at the same time I condemn, reject, and anathematize everything that is contrary to those propositions, and all heresies without exception that have been condemned, rejected, and anathematized by the Church. I, _____, promise, vow, and swear that, with God's help, I shall most constantly hold and profess this true Catholic faith, outside which no one can be saved and which I now freely profess and truly hold. With the help of God, I shall profess it whole and unblemished to my dying breath; and, To the best of my ability, I shall see to it that my subjects or those entrusted to me by virtue of my office hold it, teach it, and preach it. So help me God and His holy Gospel."[353]

---

351 The Sources Of Catholic Dogma, # 998, Page: 303
352 The Sources Of Catholic Dogma, # 999, Page: 303
353 [The words in parentheses in this paragraph are now inserted into the Tridentine profession of faith by order of Pope Pius IX in a decree issued by the Holy Office, January 20, 1877 (Acta Sanctae Sedis, X [1877], 71 ff.).] (DZ 1000.)

Oath Against the Errors of Modernism

I, _____, firmly embrace and accept all and each of the things defined, affirmed and declared by the inerrant Magisterium of the Church, mainly those points of doctrine directly opposed to the errors of our time. And in the first place I profess that God, beginning and end of all things, can be certainly known, and therefore also proved, as the cause through its effects, by the natural light of reason through the things that have been made, that is, through the visible works of creation.

Secondly, I admit and recognize as most certain signs of the divine origin of the Christian religion the external arguments of revelation, that is, the divine deeds, and in the first place the miracles and prophecies. And I maintain that these are eminently suited to the mentality of all ages and men, including those of our time.

Thirdly, I also firmly believe that the Church, guardian and teacher of the revealed word, was immediately and directly instituted by the real and historical Christ himself, while dwelling with us; and that it was built upon Peter, prince of the apostolic hierarchy, and his successors till the end of time.

Fourthly, I sincerely accept the doctrine of the faith handed on to us by the Apostles through the orthodox Fathers, always with the same meaning and interpretation; and therefore I flatly reject the heretical invention of the evolution of dogmas, to the effect that these would change their meaning from that previously held by the Church. I equally condemn every error whereby the divine deposit, handed over to the Spouse of Christ to be faithfully kept by her, would be replaced by a philosophical invention or a creation of human consciousness, slowly formed by the effort of men and to be henceforward perfected by an indefinite progress.

Fifthly, I maintain in all certainty and sincerely profess that faith is not a blind feeling of religion welling up from the recesses of the subconscious, by the pressure of the heart and of the inclination of the morally educated will, but a real assent of the intellect to the truth received from outside through the ear, whereby we believe that the things said, testified and revealed by the personal God, our Creator and Lord, are true, on account of the authority of God, who is supremely truthful.

I also submit myself with due reverence, and wholeheartedly join in all condemnations, declarations and prescriptions contained in the encyclical <u>Pascendi</u> and in the decree <u>Lamentabili</u>, mainly those concerning the so-called history of dogmas.

Likewise I reprove the error of those who affirm that the faith proposed by the Church can be repugnant to history, and that the Catholic dogmas, in the way they are understood now, cannot accord with the truer origins of the Christian religion. I also condemn and reject the opinion of those who say that the more learned Christian has a two-fold personality, one of the believer and the other of the historian, as if it would be lawful for the historian to uphold views which are in contradiction with the faith of the believer, or to lay down propositions from which it would follow that the dogmas are false or doubtful, as long as these dogmas were not directly denied. I likewise reprove the method of judging and interpreting Holy Scripture which consists in ignoring the tradition of the Church, the analogy of faith and the rulings of the Apostolic See, following the opinions of rationalists, and not only unlawfully but recklessly upholding the critique of the text as the only and supreme rule.

Besides, I reject the opinion of those who maintain that whoever teaches theological history, or writes about these matters, has to set aside beforehand any preconceived opinion regarding the supernatural origin of Catholic tradition, as well as the divine promise of a help for the perpetual preservation of each one of the revealed truths; and that, besides, the writings of each of the Fathers should be interpreted only by the principles of science, leaving aside all sacred authority, and with the freedom of judgment wherewith any secular monument is usually studied.

Lastly, I profess myself in everything totally averse to the error whereby modernists hold that there is nothing divine in sacred tradition, or, what is much worse, that there is, but in a pantheistic sense; so that nothing remains there but the bare and simple fact to be equated to the common facts of history, namely, some men who through their work, skill and ingenuity, continue in subsequent ages the school started by Christ and his apostles. Therefore I most firmly retain the faith of the Fathers, and will retain it up to the last gasp of my life, regarding the unwavering charisma of the truth, which exists, has existed and will always exist in the succession of bishops from the Apostles; not so that what is maintained is what may appear better or more suitably adapted to the culture of each age, but so that the absolute and unchangeable truth preached by the Apostles from the beginning may never be believed or understood otherwise.

All these things I pledge myself to keep faithfully, integrally and sincerely, and to watch over them without fail, never moving away from them whether in teaching or in any way by word or in writing. Thus do I promise, thus do I swear, so help me God, etc.

Appendices

The following documents are provided to support the information above, because they are not readily available or the version readily available has deficiencies. All are referred to above and the references can be found in the Index at the end of this work.

Cum Ex Apostolatus Officio
The Bull of Pope Paul IV Against Heretics

PAUL, Bishop, Servant of the Servants of God, for the perpetual remembrance hereof:

Since, by reason of the office of the Apostolate to us (though without our deserts) divinely entrusted, the general cure of the flock of the Lord devolves to us; and we are accordingly bound like a vigilant shepherd to watch assiduously and to provide attentively for its faithful protection, and salutary direction in order that those who in this age (our sins occasioning it) leaning on their own wisdom rebel against the teaching of the orthodox faith with greater license and injury than is wont, and with their superstitions and fictitious inventions perverting the meaning of the holy Scriptures, endeavor to rend the unity of the Catholic Church and the seamless robe of the Lord, should be driven from the fold of Christ, and should not remain teachers of error while they refuse to become disciples of the truth.

§1. We considering a matter of this kind to be of so grave and perilous a nature that even the Roman Pontiff, who is the viceregent of God and the Lord Jesus Christ upon Earth, having a plenitude of power over nations and kingdoms, judging all and being judged of none in this present world, may nevertheless be reproved if he is found deviating from the faith-and (considering moreover) that where there is greater danger there should be also a fuller and more diligent consultation, lest false prophets or others having secular jurisdiction also, should entangle miserably the souls of the faithful, and should draw down with them into perdition and destruction the innumerable peoples committed to their charge and government in spiritual or temporal matters, and so it might happen that we should see the Abomination of Desolation spoken of by Daniel the Prophet, in the holy place. We therefore desiring as far as with God's help we can, in virtue of our pastoral office, to capture the foxes who seek to destroy the Lord's vineyard and to drive the wolves from the fold; lest we should seem like dumb dogs unwilling to bark and be compared to bad husbandmen and mercenaries.

§2. Having had mature deliberation with our venerable brethren the Cardinals of the Holy Roman Church, by their advice and unanimous assent, approve and renew, by our Apostolic authority, all and singular sentences, censures and penalties of excommunication, suspension, and interdict, privation, and every other such sentence made by every one of the Roman Pontiffs our predecessors, and held and received as such by their Extravagants, or ordained by the sacred councils received by the Church of God, or by the decrees and statutes of the holy Fathers, and Apostolic Canons, constitutions and ordinances against heretics and Schismatics, and ordain that they shall be perpetually observed, and out to be, and shall be renewed in all their freshness if they have fallen into disuse. Also (we decree) that all persons whatsoever who shall be found or confess or be convicted as guilty of having deviated from the Catholic faith, or fallen into any heresy, or to have incurred, executed or committed any schism, or who (which God of his mercy forbid) shall in future wander from the faith, fall into heresy, or incur the guilt of schism, or shall be found or confess or be convicted to have done so, of whatever state, degree, order, condition and preeminence he may be, even if he shall be distinguished by Episcopal, Archepiscopal, Patriarchal, Primatial, or any other greater dignities of the Church, or the Cardinalitial or Legatine authority, or by any worldly dignity as those of Count, baron, Marquis, Duke, King, or Emperor, all and every of these we will and decree shall incur the aforesaid sentences, censures and pains.

§3 And, furthermore, considering that it is meet that those who do not abstain from such evils from the love of virtue, should be deterred from them by the fear of punishment, and that Bishops, Archbishops, Cardinals, Legates, Counts, etc., Kings and Emperors, who ought to teach and be a good example to others that they may be retained in the Catholic faith, sin more grievously than others inasmuch as they not only lose themselves, but draw down with them innumerable peoples confided to their care and government into perdition and the pit of destruction, by the same advice and assent and by this constitution of perpetual validity, in hatred of so great a crime, than which none can be greater in the Church of God or more pernicious, in the plenitude of our power, we sanction, decree, declare, and define that while all the aforesaid sentences, censures, etc. shall remain in their force and efficacy, and be carried out in their result, all and singular Bishops, etc...Dukes, Kings and Emperors who hitherto shall be found, confess or be convicted of deviating from the faith, of falling into heresy or of incurring, exciting or committing a schism...since in this they are the more inexcusable than others, beyond the sentences, censures and penalties aforesaid, shall ipso facto without any process of law or proof of fact, be deprived of their orders, cathedrals, churches, cardinalitial and legatine honors...and of their dignities as Counts, Barons, Marquises, Dukes, Kings and Emperors, altogether and absolutely, and shall be in future held to be disqualified and incapable, and shall be deemed as relapsed and condemned in everything and by all means, even if they shall have previously publicly abjured their heresy nor shall they be ever restored to their previous state, or redintegrated or rehabilated in their bishoprics, etc...Duchies, Kingdoms, and Empires. Nay further they shall be left to the will of the secular power to be punished with due severity; unless, in the case of worthy proofs of a true repentance being found in them and the fruits thereof, through the benignity and clemency of this See, it may see fit to relegate them to some monastery or other place of regular monks, to carry on a perpetual penance in the bread of sorrow and water of affliction; and they shall be held, treated and reputed by all of every condition as relapsed persons, and as such shall be avoided and deprived of all human consolations.

§4 And all who claim the rights of patronage and of nominating fit persons for cathedral, metropolitical and patriarchal churches or other ecclesiastical benefices vacant by reason of the privation aforesaid (in order that such churches may not be exposed to disadvantage from a prolonged vacancy but may be redeemed from the slavery of heretics, and granted to fit persons who may faithfully lead the people in the paths of righteousness) shall be bound to present to such churches, etc., other fit persons within the period assigned by law or by concordats or compacts entered into with our said See, either by ourselves or by the Roman Pontiff at the time existing, in respect of such presentation; otherwise, such time having elapsed, the full and free disposition of the said benefices shall devolve to us or to the said Roman Pontiff in full right.

§5 And further, those who shall in any way knowingly presume to receive, defend, favor, or give credit to persons thus taken, confessed, or convicted, or to propagate their doctrines, shall incur the sentence of excommunication ipso facto, and shall be accounted infamous, nor shall they be admitted by voice, or person, writings, representatives, or proctors to public or private offices or councils, synods, general or provincial Councils, nor to the Conclave of Cardinals, nor any congregation of the faithful, nor to the election of anyone, nor to give evidence; they shall be unable to make a will or to inherit under a will, nor shall any be compelled to respond to them in regard to any matter of business. But if perchance they should happen to be judges, their sentences shall be null and void, nor shall any causes be brought to their hearing; if they should be advocates, their advocacy shall not be admitted; if writers, the documents drawn up by them shall be of none effect or authority. And furthermore, the clergy shall be deprived ipso facto of all and singular churches, dignities and offices ecclesiastical, however they may be qualified for them, if they are obtained in any form from such persons; and both they and the laity, however qualified and endowed with any of the said dignities whatever, shall be deprived ipso facto of the kingdoms, dukedoms, dominions, feuds; and temporal goods possessed by them; and their kingdoms, dukedoms, dominions, feuds, and all their goods whatsoever shall be confiscated, and shall become the right and property of those who shall first occupy them, provided they remain in the sincere faith and unity of the Holy Roman Church, and in the obedience of ourselves, and of our canonical appointed successors.

§6 We add moreover that if at any time it shall appear that any Bishop even if he assert for himself the rank of Archbishop, Patriarch, Primate, or Cardinal of the aforesaid Roman Church, or legate, **or even Roman Pontiff before his promotion or assumption into the Cardinalate or Pontificate, shall have deviated from the Catholic faith or have fallen into any heresy, or incurred, excited or committed any schism, his promotion or assumption even made in full concord and with the unanimous consent of all the Cardinals, shall be null, abrogated, and void, nor shall be called or become valid even by the reception of the grace of consecration nor the subsequent possession of government and administration, nor even by the enthronization or adoration of the elected person as Roman Pontiff or the universal obedience rendered to him for how long a period soever.** Nor shall he be held legitimate in any form, nor be deemed capable of giving or be held to have given any authority of administration in things spiritual or temporal to any person promoted to bishoprics, etc., or assumed to the Cardinalate or to the Roman Pontificate. But all and everything said, done, acted and administered by persons thus chosen and all things resulting therefrom shall be without force, and no firmness or legal right shall be assigned to them; and those who are thus promoted and assumed shall without any authoritative declaration be deprived of every dignity, place, honor, title, office and power.

§7 And it shall be lawful for all who are thus promoted and assumed, if they have not deviated from the faith, nor become heretics, nor incurred, excited, nor committed a schism, and to their dependents, both secular and regular, clergy and laity, and even to the Cardinals, who have been present at the election of such Pontiff who has previously deviated from the faith or become heretical or schismatical, or have otherwise consented to his election and given him obedience and adoration, and are bound to such promoted persons by homage or oath or caution...to recede with immunity from the obedience and devotion to those thus promoted or assumed, and to avoid them as ethnics, publicans and heresiarchs those who are released from such obedience remaining nevertheless bound to give fidelity and obedience to the future Bishops, Archbishops, Patriarchs, Primates, and Cardinals, and to the Roman Pontiff canonically elected. And for the greater confusion of those thus (unlawfully) promoted and assumed, should they wish to continue their government and administration, it shall be lawful to invoke the secular arm against them, and those who withdraw from their obedience by reason of the circumstances already described, shall not be liable to any punishment by censure or otherwise, as rending the seamless robe of Christ.

§8 And this notwithstanding all constitutions and ordinances Apostolic, privileges, indults and letters Apostolic... even given motu proprio, Ex certa scientia, and in the plenitude of Apostolic power; or granted consistorially or in any other form whatever; though they may have been approved and renewed many times over, and incorporated in the body of the law. Notwithstanding also any capitulars of the conclave however ratified by oath or Apostolic confirmation, and sworn to by ourselves. All the above constitutions by these presents, (assuming the contents to be here expressed and inserted word for word) we ratify in all points, except only in this instance, in which we expressly and specially derogate from them, and in all things whatever which are not contrary to this exception.

§9 And that this letter may become known to all whom it concerns, we will that it, or a copy of it subscribed by the hand of a notary public, and sealed by some dignitary of the Church, (to which copy we will that full credit shall be given,) shall be published and affixed on the doors of the Basilica of the Prince of the Apostles in the City, and of the Apostolic Chancery, and at the entrance of the Campo di Fiora, by some of our Cursors, and that the affixing such copy and the proof of it being so affixed, shall suffice and be held as a solemn and legal publication, and that none other shall be required or expected.

§10 Let it therefore be legal for no one to infringe or rashly to attempt to contravene this instrument of our approbation, innovation, sanction, statute, derogation, will and decree. If however anyone shall presume to make such attempt, let him know that he will incur the indignation of Almighty God, and of the blessed Apostles Peter and Paul.

Given at Rome, at Saint Peter's, in the year of our Lord's incarnation, 1558, on the 15th of the Kalends of March (February 14th), in the fourth year of our Pontificate.

(Signed) BARENGUS

Insauratio Liturgica

Declaration on the meaning of translations of sacramental formulae S.C.D.F., insauratio Liturgica, 25 January 1974

The liturgical reform which has been carried out in accordance with the Constitution of the Second Vatican Council has made certain changes in the essential formulae of the sacramental rites. These new expressions, like the other ones, have had to be translated into modern languages in such a way that the original sense finds expression in the idiom proper to each language. This has given rise to certain difficulties, which have come to light now that the translations have been sent by episcopal, conferences to the Holy See for approve. In these circumstances, the Sacred Congregation for the Doctrine of the Faith again calls attention to the necessity that the essential formulae of the sacramental rites render faithfully the original sense of the Latin "typical text." With that in mind it declares:

When a vernacular translation of a sacramental formula is submitted to the Holy See for approval, it examines it carefully. When it is satisfied that it expresses the meaning, intended by the Church, it approves and confirms it, stipulating, however, that it must be understood in accordance with the mind of the Church as expressed in the original Latin text.

Holiness, Pope Paul VI, in the audience granted to the Cardinal Prefect on the 25th day of January, 1974, gave his approval.

AAS 66-661; Sacred Congregation of the Doctrine of the Faith, declaration, 25 January, 1974. Annotations in Notitiae, 10 (1974), 396-397.

Catechism of the Council of Trent

"The form of the consecration of the wine, the other element of this Sacrament is, for the reasons assigned with regard to the bread, necessary to be accurately known, and clearly understood by the priest. It is firmly to be believed that the form of consecrating the chalice is comprehended in these words: "This is the chalice of My Blood of the new and eternal testament: the mystery of faith: which shall be shed for you and for many to the remission of sins." These words are for the most part taken from Scripture. Some of them, however, have been preserved in the Church by apostolic tradition. The words "this is the chalice" are taken from Saint Luke (22:20), and are also mentioned by the Apostle. (I Corinthians 11:25) The words that immediately follow, "of My Blood, or My Blood of the new testament, which shall be shed for you, and for many to the remission of sins," are taken in part from Saint Luke, and in part from Saint Matthew. (Matthew 26:28)

"The additional words, "for you and for many," are taken, some from Saint Matthew and some from Saint Luke, and under the guidance of the Spirit of God, combined together by the Catholic Church. They serve emphatically to designate the fruit and advantage of His Passion, we believe that the Redeemer shed His Blood, for the salvation of all men; but looking to the advantages, which mankind derive from its efficacy, we find, at once, that they are not extended to the whole, but to a large proportion of the human race. When, therefore, our Lord said: "for you", He meant either those who were present, of those whom He had chosen from among the Jews, amongst whom were, with the exception of Judas, all His disciples with whom He then conversed; but when He adds, "for many" He would include the remainder of the elect from amongst the Jews and Gentiles. With great propriety therefore, were the words, for all omitted, because here the fruit of the Passion is alone spoken of, and to the elect only did His Passion bring the fruit of salvation.

January 1970 Notice From Rome

In some vernacular versions the words of the formula for the consecration of the wine **pro multis** are translated in the following way: in English **for all men**; in Spanish **por todos** and in Italian **per tutti**.

The following is asked:

a) Is there a good reason, and if there is, what is it, for deciding on such a variation?

b) Whether the doctrine regarding this matter handed down through the Roman Catechism ordered by Decree of the Council of Trent and edited by Saint Pius V is to be held outdated?

c) Whether the versions of the above mentioned biblical text are to be held less appropriate?

d) Whether in the approval given to this vernacular variation in the liturgical text something less correct crept in, and which now requires correction or amending?

Response: The above variation is fully justified:

a) According to exegetes, the Aramaic word which in Latin is translated **pro multis**, means **pro omnibus**: the multitude for whom Christ died is unbounded, which is the same as saying: Christ died for all. Saint Augustine will help recall this: "You see what He hath given; find out then what He bought. The Blood of Christ was the price. What is equal to this? What, but the whole world? What, but all nations? They are very ungrateful for their price, or very proud, who say that the price is so small that it bought the Africans only; or that they are so great, as that it was given for them alone." (Enarr. In Ps. 95, n. 5)

b) In no way is the doctrine of the Roman Catechism to be held outdated: the distinction that the death of Christ was sufficient for all, efficacious only for many, still holds its value.

c) In the approval given to this vernacular variation in the liturgical text, nothing less than correct has crept in, which would require correction or amendment.

May 1970 Notice from Rome

A response was already given in Notitiae, n. 50 (January 1970), pp. 39-40, to the difficulty that in the vernacular interpretations of the words of the consecration of the wine **pro omnibus** was used in place of **pro multis**. Since, however, some uneasiness seems to persist, it seemed that the matter should be addressed again a little more extensively from an exegetical point of view.

In that response, one reads: According to exegetes the Aramaic word, which in Latin is translated **pro multis**, means **pro omnibus**. This assertion should be expressed a little more cautiously. To be exact: In the Hebrew (Aramaic) language there is one word for **omnes** and another for **multi**. The word **multi** then, strictly speaking, does not mean **omnes**.

But because the word **multi** in different ways in our Western languages does not exclude the whole, it can and does in fact connote it, where the context or subject matter suggests or requires it. It is not easy to offer clear examples of this phenomenon. Here are some:

In 3 Esdras [Ezra] 8:3 we read: "Many have been created, but only a few shall be saved." It is clear that all have been created. But here the interest is not in the whole, but in the opposite of **few**. Hence, **many** is used, when it truth it means **all**.

In the Qumram text Hodayot IV, 28, 29, both words **many** and **all** are found in a synonymous parallel (two parallel verses in which the same thing is said twice): "You have worked wonders among the many on account of your glory that you might make known to all your great works."

Moreover, in Qumram **many** (with or without the article) came to be a technical term (almost a name) for the community of all the full fledged members, and thus just in the **rule** of the sect it occurs in around 30 places.

We come now to the texts of the New Testament with which we are particularly concerned: Romans 5:12,15. Here the comparative argumentation from the minor premise to the major is set up between the universality of Adam's sin and the universality of Christ's grace: Therefore, just as sin came into the world through one man, and death came through sin, and so death spread to all because all have sinned (after the insertion of verses 13 and 14, the comparison continues) But the free gift is not like the trespass. For if the many died through the one man's trespass, much more surely have the grace of God and the free gift in the grace of the one man, Jesus Christ, abounded for the many. Let us note: **all** those of the first part become the **many** (with an article) of the second part. Just as sin affects all, or rather much more, so also grace is destined for all.

Mark 10:45 = Matthew 20:28 has Jesus' words: "the Son of Man came not to be served but to serve, and to give His life a ransom for many." That **for many** ambiguous in itself, in fact is to be understood as **for all**, proven by what we read in 1 Timothy 2:6: "Christ Jesus, who gave Himself a ransom for all."

But even if we didn't have this authoritative interpretation, that for many' nonetheless should certainly be understood as **for all** because the coming of Jesus ("He came in order to give...") is explicitly carried out for the purpose which can abundantly be shown to have as its object the whole world, i.e. the human race as a whole.

John 1:29: "Here is the Lamb of God who takes away the sin of the world!"

John 3:16,17: "For God so loved the world that he gave his only Son, so that everyone who believes in him...may have eternal life. Indeed, God did not send the Son into the world to condemn the world, but in order that the world might be saved through him."

1 John 2:2: "He is the atoning sacrifice for our sins, and not for ours only but also for the sins of the whole world."

1 John 4:14: "And we have seen and do testify that the Father has sent his Son as the Savior of the world."

1 Timothy 4:10: "...We have our hope set on the living God, who is the Savior of all people, especially of those who believe."

These texts, however, have the Eucharist itself in view:

John 6:33: "For the bread of God is that which comes down from Heaven and gives life to the world."

John 6:51: "The bread that I will give for the life of the world is my flesh."

Given all this, it can indeed rightly be asked, not so much what the words **pro multis** in the consecration mean, but rather given all this evidence, why **pro omnibus** is not explicitly said.

In response, it seems that

1) in the primitive Palestinian Church, considering both their soteriology and their Semitic mind set, there was no misunderstanding that had to be avoided by employing the formula **pro omnibus**. They could freely keep the traditional **pro multis** because those Christians sensed and marveled at the beauty of that original formula **pro multis**.

2) **pro multis** seems to have been used by Jesus himself, because evoking the memory of Chapter 53 of Isaiah about the Servant of Yahweh who sacrifices himself, it is suggested that Jesus would fulfill what was predicted about the Servant of Yahweh. The main text is Isaiah 53:11b-12: "The righteous one, my servant, shall make many righteous, and he shall bear their iniquities. Therefore I will allot him a portion with the great, and he shall divide the spoil with the strong; because he poured out himself to death...; yet he bore the sin of many, and made intercession for the transgressors."

Therefore the formula **pro multis** instead of **pro omnibus** in our texts (Mark 10:45 = Matthew 20:28; Mark 14:24 = Matthew 26:28) seems to be due to the desired allusion to the Servant of Yahweh whose work Jesus carried out by his death.

This brings us now to another question: Why therefore in our liturgical version this venerable original **pro multis** should yield to the phrase **pro omnibus**? I respond: because of a certain accidental but true inconvenience: the phrase **for many** -- as it is said -- in our minds (not forewarned) excludes that universality of the redemptive work which for the Semitic mind could be and certainly was connoted in that phrase because of the theological context. However, the allusion to the theology of the Servant of Yahweh, however eloquent for the ancients, among us is clear only to the experts.

But if on the other hand it is said that the phrase **for all** also has its own inconvenience, because for some it might suggest that all will actually be saved, the danger of such an erroneous understanding is estimated to hardly exist among Catholics.

Besides, the change which the words of the consecration underwent was not unique nor the first. For the traditional Latin text already combines the Lucan text **pro vobis** with the phrase of Mark and Matthew **pro multis**. And that is not the first change. For already the liturgy of the early Church (Mark-Matthew) seems to have adjusted the saying over the chalice to the formula pronounced over the bread. For originally that formula of the chalice according to Paul (1 Corinthians 11:25) and Luke (22:20) was: "This cup that is poured out for you is the new covenant in my blood." -- a formula which was excellent perhaps in depth, but not really in clarity.

It is clear how the Church of the Apostles was not interested in preserving the very voice of the Lord even in the words of the consecration, certainly cited for the first time as such by Jesus himself.

Monseigneur, We Do Not Want This Peace
By Fr. Guerard des Lauriers O.P.

You celebrated the **innovated Mass** from the beginning of April 1969 until 24th December 1971.

On 5th May 1969 some friends who held you in high esteem, among whom was the signatory of these lines, had come to be present at the Mass which you celebrated at the altar where lie the remains of Saint Pius V in the Roman basilica of Saint Mary Major. Astonishment, scandal and grief! Upon the very tomb of Saint Pius V it was the **innovated Mass** which you celebrated! On the way out, you were confronted on the piazza by a respectful, though sorrowful, enquiry to which you declared. "If Mgr. Lefebvre were seen to celebrate the traditional Mass there would be danger of scandal."

To these same friends who were labouring with your encouragement on the elaboration of the text which later became the Letter of Cardinals Bacci and Ottaviani[354], you gave comforting assurances: "We shall have six hundred bishops." That was certainly something to convince the Pope! Well...there was not a single Bishop, not one, and not even you. In fact, in reality, you were more concerned about **not giving scandal** than about defending the truth.

You continued to celebrate the **innovated Mass** at Fribourg and at Econe. The initial hopes bore fruit nevertheless, Bernard Tissier, de Malleray, Paul Aulagnier, Bernard Waltz and three others. On Christmas Day at the end of lunch, the Dominican Father whose signature is below and who was then staying at Econe remarked, with gentle irony, "Monseigneur, it is a pity that, while maintaining Tradition, you have been celebrating something called a **New Mass** which is not the Mass of Tradition." This simple remark really set the house on fire. The **six**, all your living hope exploded. Each in his way, and all together repeated the same message to you: "How is it possible

---

354   More formally known as the Ottaviani Intervention.

to establish fidelity to Tradition on a **Mass** which was **innovated** in opposition to Tradition?" The incident was very vehement and, moreover, quickly closed. On that night of 24-25th December 1971 at the Midnight Mass, to the great joy of everyone, you returned to the rite promulgated by Saint Pius V.

    Maundy Thursday
    (signed) Guerard des Lauriers O.P.
    12th April 1979
    for a group of the faithful who cling to tradition.
    In memoriam, Maundy Thursday 3rd April 1969.
    the date of the promulgation of the Novus Ordo. (Translator).

Declaration of Archbishop Peter Martin Ngo-Dihn Thuc

How does the Catholic Church appear today as we look at it? In Rome, John Paul II reigns as **Pope**, surrounded by the body of Cardinals and of many bishops and prelates. Outside of Rome, the Catholic Church seems to be flourishing, along with its bishops and priests. The number of Catholics is great. Daily the Mass is celebrated in so many churches, and on Sundays the churches are full of many faithful who come to hear the Mass and receive Holy Communion. But in the sight of God, how does today's Church appear? Are the Masses both the daily ones and those at which people assist on Sundays pleasing to God? By no means, because that Mass is the same for Catholics as it is for Protestants therefore it is displeasing to God and invalid. The only Mass that pleases God is the Mass of Saint Pius V, which is offered by few priests and bishops, among whom I count myself. Therefore, to the extent that I can, I will open seminaries for educating candidates for that priesthood which is pleasing to God. Besides this **Mass**, which does not please God, there are many other things that God rejects: for example, changes in the ordination of priests, the consecration of bishops, and in the Sacraments of Confirmation and of Extreme Unction. Moreover, the **priests** now hold to: 1) Modernism; 2) false Ecumenism 3) the adoration [or cult] of man; 4) the freedom to embrace any religion whatsoever; 5) the unwillingness to condemn heresies and to expel the heretics. Therefore, in so far as I am a bishop of the Roman Catholic Church, I judge that the See of the Catholic Church in Rome to be vacant; and it is necessary for me, as bishop, to do all that is needed so that the Catholic Church in Rome endures for the eternal salvation of souls.

February 25, 1982
Munich
+Peter Martin Ngo-dinh-Thuc
Archbishop
1. Quo Primum
2. The Council of Trent, Session XXII. (This session

forbade wandering priests to say mass, unless first proving themselves faithful and gave as its reasoning the reverence owed to the Mass.)

    3. <u>Adorabili Eucharisti</u> of Pius VII; Decree for the Armenians, Council of Florence.[355]

    4. <u>Missale Romanum</u> of Pius V; De defectibus formal (found in the Missale Romanum.)

    5. <u>Auctorem Fidei</u> of Pius VI;[356] <u>Lamentabili</u> of Pius X; <u>Pascendi Domenici Gregis</u> of Pius X.[357]

    6. <u>Quanta Cura</u> of Pius IX;[358] <u>Unam Sanctam</u>, of Boniface VIII.[359]

    7. Canon 1322.[360]

    8. <u>Cum Ex Apostolatus</u> of Paul IV; Code of Canon Law, Canon 188, No. 4.

    9.   <u>Pontificale Romanum</u>; <u>De Consecratione Electi in Episcopum</u>; "Forma Juramenti" et "Examen."

---

355   <u>The Sources Of Catholic Dogma</u>, # 698, Pages: 222
        <u>The Sources Of Catholic Dogma</u>, # 715, Pages: 230
356   <u>The Sources Of Catholic Dogma</u>, # 1501-1599, Pages: 370-398
357   <u>The Sources Of Catholic Dogma</u>, # 2001-2109, Pages: 508-541
358   <u>The Sources Of Catholic Dogma</u>, # 1700-1780, Pages: 433-442
359   <u>The Sources Of Catholic Dogma</u>, # 468-469, Pages: 186-187
360   <u>A Practical Commentary On The Code Of Canon Law</u>, Volume 2, Canon 1322, Page: 107

Bibliography

Abbott, Walter M, <u>The Documents of Vatican II</u>, New York, Guild Press, 1966.

Angles, Ramon, <u>25th Anniversary of the Founding of the SSPX</u>, January 1999, <u>The Angelus</u>, Kansas City.

Aquinas, Saint Thomas, <u>Catena Aurea: Commentary on the Four Gospels</u>, Albany, New York, Preserving Christian Publications, 1993.

Aquinas, Saint Thomas, <u>Summa Theologica</u>, volume three, Westminster, Maryland, Christian Classics, 1981.

Attwater, Donald, <u>A Catholic Dictionary</u>, New York, The Macmillan Company, 1961.

Augustine, Charles OSB DD, <u>A Commentary on the New Code of Canon Law</u>, Volume I, London, B. Herder, 1918.

Baigent, Michael; Leigh, Richard and Lincoln, Henry, <u>Holy Blood-Holy Grail</u>, New York, delacourt Press, 1982.

Barthas, Chanoine C; Da Fonseca, G SJ, <u>Our Lady of Light</u>, Milwaukee, The Bruce Publishing company, 1947.

Benns, T Stanfill and Bawden, David, <u>Will the Catholic Church Survive the Twentieth Century?</u>, Belvue, Kansas, Christ the King Library, 1990.

Berry, E Sylvester, <u>The Apocalypse of St. John</u>, Columbus, Ohio, John W. Winterich, 1921.

Bouscaren, T. Lincoln SJ AM LLB STD, <u>The Canon Law Digest</u> volume III, Milwaukee, The Bruce Publishing company, 1953.

Bouscaren, T. Lincoln SJ AM LLB STD and O'Connor, SJ, AM STL JCD, <u>The Canon Law Digest</u> volume V, Milwaukee, The Bruce Publishing company, 1963.

Bouscaren, T. Lincoln, <u>The Updated Church: a Conservative's Comment</u>, April 1965, <u>Homiletic and Pastoral Review.</u>

Callan, Charles J OP and Mchugh, John a OP, <u>A Parochial Course of Doctrinal Instructions for all Sundays and Holydays of the Year; Based on the Teachings of the Catechism of the Council of Trent and Harmonized with the Gospels and Epistles of the Sundays and Feasts</u>, New York, B. Herder, 1920.

Cicognani, Amleto Giovanni, <u>Canon Law</u>, Philadelphia, The Dolphin Press, 1935.

Coomaraswamy, Rama, <u>The Destruction of the Christian Tradition</u>, Bloomington, Indiana, World Wisdom, 2006

Coppens, Charles SJ, <u>A Systematic Study of the Catholic Religion</u>, St. Louis, B. Herder Book Company, 1917.

Culleton, R. Gerald, <u>The Prophets and Our Times</u>, Rockford, Illinois, TAN, 1974.

Cuneo, Michael W, <u>The Smoke of Satan</u>, Baltimore, The Johns Hopkins University Press, 1999.

Davies, Michael, <u>Apologia Pro Marcel Lefebvre: Part I 1905-1976</u>, Dickinson, Texas, The Angelus Press, 1979.

de Ligouri, Saint Alphonsus, The Holy Eucharist, Brooklyn, Redemptorist Fathers, 1934.

de Ligouri, Saint Alphonsus, The Holy Mass, New York, Benzinger Brothers, 1889.

de Sales, Saint Francis, The Catholic Controversy, Rockford, Illinois, TAN, 1989.

Deharbe, Joseph, translated by Fander, John, A Full Catechism of the Catholic Religion, Hawthorne, California, Christian Book Club of America, 1924.

Denzinger, translated by Deferrari, Roy J, The Sources of Catholic Dogma, Fitzwilliam, NH, Loreto Publications, 2007.

Donovan, J, The Catechism of the Council of Trent, New York, Christian press Association Publishing Company, 1905.

Emerton, Ephraim, The Correspondence of Pope Gregory VII, New York, Columbia University Press, 1932.

Eudes, Saint John, translated by Di Targiani, Charles and Hauser, Ruth, The Admirable Heart of Mary, New York, P. J. Kenedy & Sons, 1948.

Eudes, Saint John, The Life and the Kingdom of Jesus in Christian Souls, New York, P. J. Kenedy & Sons, 1945.

Eudes, Saint John, translated by Murphy, W Leo, The Priest: His Dignity and Obligations, New York, P. J. Kenedy & Sons, 1947.

Flannery, Austin OP, Vatican Council II The Conciliar and Post Cocliar Documents 1981 Edition, Northport, New York, Costello Publishing Company, 1980.

Friedl, Phil, History of the Church: The Formation of the Apostles of the Latter Times, Delia, St. Pius X Press, 2009.

Goffine, Leonard, translated from the German by Pilz, Gerard OSB, Explanation of the Epistles and Gospels for the Sundays, Holydays and Festivals throughout the Ecclesiastical Year to which are added the Lives of Many Saints, New York, Fr. Pustet & C., 1880.

International Commission on English in the Liturgy, The Rites of the Catholic Church, New York, Pueblo Publishing Company, 1976.

Journet, Charles, The Church of the Word Incarnate, Great Britain, Purnell and Sons, 1954

Kinkead, Thomas L, An Explanantion of the Baltimore Catechism, Rockford, Illinois, TAN, 1988.

Manning, Henry Cardinal, The Pastoral Office, Delia, St. Pius X Press, 2010.

Montini, John the Baptist, Romano Pontifice Eligendo, www2.fiu.edu, 1975.

O'Reilly, Edmund J SJ, The Relations of the Church to Society, London, John Hodges, 1892

Panakal, Francis, The Man of Sin, Montreal, Bandia-Roo, 1983.

Parsons, Reuben DD, Studies in Church History, volume II, Philadelphia, John Joseph McVey, 1909.

Pospishil, Victor J JCD, Code of Oriental Canon Law: The Law of Persons, Ford City, PA, St. Mary's Ukrainian Catholic Church, 1960.

Ratzinger Milestones quote
http://www.losangelesmission.com/ed/articles/2000/0400cr.htm

In Dominico Agro Pope Clement XIII

Roche, Msgr. Georges, <u>Pie XII Devant L'Histoire</u>, Paris: Editions, Robert Lafont, 1972

Roncalli, Angelo, <u>Mission to France</u>, New York, McGraw-Hill, 1966.

Schaff, Philip DD LLD, <u>Nicene and Post-Nicene Fathers: Volume 13: First Series</u>, Reabady, Massachusettes, Hendrickson, 1994.

Schaff, Philip DD LLD, <u>Nicene and Post-Nicene Fathers: Volume 4: Second Series</u>, Reabady, Massachusettes, Hendrickson, 1994.

Schomger, K E CSSR, <u>Life of Anna Catherine Emmerich</u>, volume II, Rockford, Illinois, TAN, 1976.

Schroeder, H. J., <u>Disciplinary Decrees of the General Councils</u>, St. Louis, B Herder Book Co., 1937.

http://sedevacantist.com/forums/viewtopic.php?f=2&t=10&view=next

<u>The Code of Canon Law</u>, Canon Law Society of Great Britain and Ireland, Collins, 1983.

http://www.traditioninaction.org/religious/n009rp_HomosexualPriests.htm

Trinchard, Paul, <u>Guidelines for Going Outside the Church for</u>

Mass and Confession, Metarie, Louisianna, Maeta, 2000.

Van de Putte, Walter CSSP LLD, Saint Pius X Daily Missal, New York, Catholic Book Publishing Company, 1956.

Vianney, Jean Baptiste Marie, Sermons for the Sundays and Feast of the Year, Long Prarie, Minnesota, Neumann Press, 1995.

Weller, Philip T, The Roman Ritual, Milwaukee, The Bruce Publishing Company, 1948.

http://www.fatimainquiry.blogspot.com/

Wikipedia, John Jay Report, http://en.wikipedia.org/wiki/John_Jay_Report,

Wilhelm, J, Councils, General in The Catholic Encyclopedia, Volume IV, New York, Robert Appleton, Company, 1908.

Wojtyla, Karol, Universi Dominici Gregis, www.vatican.va, 1996.

Woywod, Stanislaus OFM LLB, revised by Smith, Callistus OFM JCL, A Practical Commentary on the Code of Canon Law, New York, Joseph F. Wagner, Inc., 1948 in two volumes.

http://www.zenit.org/english/visualizza.phtml?sid=58517

Index

Allah as god of Vatican II Church 70, 92
Antichrist 10, 45, 73p., 97, 99p., 102pp., 122, 137, 150
Apocalypse 73, 97p., 100, 106p., 110, 154, 184
Apocatastasis 91, 93
apostasy 30, 40, 44, 108
Apostasy 35p., 109, 111
Apostolicity 146
Appendices 165
Baltimore Catechism 31, 187
baptism 159
Baptism 71, 93p., 96, 155, 160
Catholic Action 131
CMRI 114p., 124
communion of Saints 156
Communion of Saints 129
conclave 46p., 51, 53p., 139, 171
Conclave 46, 110, 138, 140, 151p., 169
confirmation 171
Confirmation 71, 160, 182
Council of Trent...11pp., 28, 33, 56, 73, 75, 81, 93, 133, 155, 159pp., 174p., 182, 185p.
Cum Ex Apostolatus Officio 33p., 38, 166
de Sales, Saint Francis 104, 186
des Lauriers, Bishop Guerard .... 115, 118p., 138, 180p.
Dolan, Bishop Daniel 125
Emmerich, Anna Catherine 104, 188
Extreme Unction 72, 160, 182
Feeney, Fr. Leonard 94
Gregory XVII 139
heresy....10, 21p., 30p., 33p., 38pp., 52, 54, 59p., 81p., 85p., 94, 102, 116, 156, 158, 167p., 170
Heresy 37, 42
home alone 130
Home Alone 128

infallibility..................................5, 17, 20p., 25, 42, 82, 85, 116, 144
Infallibility..17, 19, 21, 27
insauratio Liturgica...173
Insauratio Liturgica...173
It is the Mass that matters.....................................134
jurisdiction........................24, 30, 64, 110p., 125, 144, 148, 166
Jurisdiction..125
Le Floch..21, 116
Lefebvre, Archbishop Marcel...66, 72, 115pp., 121p., 124, 127, 139, 180, 185
Ligouri, Saint Alphonsus..............................49, 104, 185
Lyons, Council of....................................141, 149, 152
magisterium..21, 23, 27
Magisterium..20, 162
Manning, Henry Edward Cardinal........97, 104, 111, 143p., 147, 187
Mass of John XXIII...123
Mass, Indult...87, 123, 171
Mass, Novus Ordo. 66, 68, 75, 77pp., 83, 86, 88, 105, 113pp., 122pp., 139, 152, 181
Mass, Tridentine.............................61, 78, 123, 134, 136
Mediator Dei...135
Mendez, Bishop Alfred...66, 124
Meyer, Bishop Antonio de Castro........................66, 122, 127
Modernism..................................59pp., 82, 155, 162, 182
modernists..164
Modernists...36, 58, 62, 136
Montini, John the Baptist..........58p., 67, 105p., 110, 123, 135p., 187
Ngo-Dihn, Archbishop Peter Martin Ngo-Dihn Thuc.......66, 119p., 122, 124, 127, 138, 182
Notitiae...76p., 123, 173, 176
Office of Bishop..146, 148
Pascendi.......................................36, 60, 136, 163, 183
Pedophile Crisis...5, 88, 152
Pope Alexander VII...10, 42
Pope Benedict XIV......................................22, 48p., 140, 147, 158
Pope Clement XIII...11, 188

Pope Gregory XII...48, 137, 140
Pope Leo XIII...136, 146, 150
Pope Michael..151, 184
Pope Pius XII.............................27, 30, 32, 35, 51, 53, 61, 72, 135
Pope Saint Gregory VII...186
Pope Urban VI..48p., 140
Priests as co-consecrators in Episcopal Consecration................127
Protestants..52, 78, 134, 145, 182
Quo Primum..61, 113, 182
Ratzinger, Joseph..56, 83, 88, 110p., 123, 187
Roman Catechism........................12p., 15, 28, 45, 134, 146, 175
Roncalli, Angelo........................51pp., 59, 62, 110, 123, 137, 188
rosary..113
Rosary..22, 113, 128, 130
Rubricarum Instructum..61p., 121
sacramental bishop...125
Sacrosanctum Concilium..59
scapular...130
Scapular...128, 130
schismatic..31, 37, 40, 47, 68, 81, 83, 141, 170
Schismatic..32, 167
Schmitz, Old Catholic Bishop Georg..122, 127
Schuckardt, Bishop Francis...114, 124
Siri, Joseph..51, 139, 166
Society of Saint Pius V..121, 124
Society of Saint Pius X...114, 116, 121, 123
Steiner, Maria..153
Traditionalists...116p., 119, 125, 128, 130
Trinchard, Paul...125, 188
Vatican Council..................21p., 26, 31, 37, 56, 73, 151, 161, 173, 186
Vatican II.....54pp., 58pp., 62pp., 67, 69p., 73, 82pp., 91p., 110, 116, 118, 129p., 139, 145, 149, 152, 184
Will the Catholic Church Survive the Twentieth Century?......140, 152, 184
Wojtyla, Karol..121, 123, 135, 189

St. Pius X Press
Books Available

54 Years That Changed The Catholic Church	A Layman's Way To Perfection
A Treatise On Mental Prayer	Beauty A Study In Philosophy
Bernadette of Lourdes: The Only Complete Account Of Her Life Ever Published	Characteristics Of True Devotion
Conference Matter For Religious	Eternal Punishment
Extreme Unction	Golden Book Of The Commandments And Sacraments
Guide To General Confession	History Of The Church
Holiness Of Life	Holy Week Manual For Servers
Humility Of Heart	Mercy Is Forever
New Lights On Pastoral Problems	Peter's Name
Practical Method Of Reading The Breviary	Readings For Each Sunday In The Year
Readings On Fundamental Moral Theology	Saint Bernard The Twelve Degrees Of Humility And Pride
Sanctity In America	Sister Faustina Apostle Of Divine Mercy
Spiritual Maxims	St. Pius X: A Pictorial Biography
Text Book Of Gregorian Chant	The Art Of Dying Well
The Art Of Prayer	The Blessed Sacrament: The Centre Of Immutable Truth
The Christian Trumpet	The Cult Of Our Lady
The Excellence Of The Rosary	The Four Last Things: Death, Judgment, Hell, Heaven
The Four Temperaments And Perfection	The Living Presence: The Intrinsic Value Of The Blessed Sacrament

The Mirror Of The Blessed Virgin Mary And The Psalter Of Our Lady	The Pastoral Office
The Possibility Of Invincible Ignorance Of The Natural Law	The Possibility Of Invincible Ignorance Of The Natural Law
The Present Crisis Of The Holy See	The Prisoner In The Vatican: A Story Of Pope Pius IX
The Religious State	The True Story Of The Vatican Council
The Virtues Of A Religious Superior	Vocations
Will The Catholic Church Survive The Twentieth Century	

Publisher's Contact Information

St. Pius X Press   Box 74   Delia   KS   66418   USA

Contact@stpiusxpress.com   www.stpiusxpress.com

Notes: Make checks payable to **"St. Pius X Press"**.

Made in United States
Cleveland, OH
20 February 2026